Aunt Clara

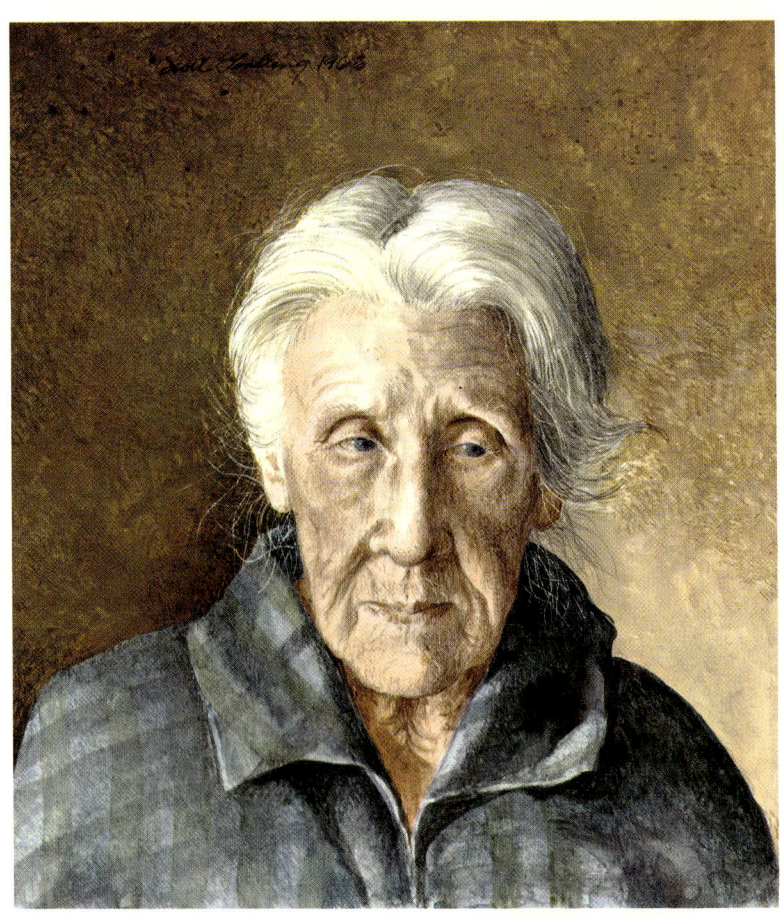

PORTRAIT OF AUNT CLARA by Scott Gentling, watercolor, 1966, 7½ x 6¾ in.

Aunt Clara

THE PAINTINGS OF CLARA McDONALD WILLIAMSON

by
Donald and Margaret Vogel

On the occasion of a retrospective exhibition
of the artist's work at the Amon Carter Museum
of Western Art, Fort Worth; the Oklahoma Art
Center, Oklahoma City; the Marion Koogler McNay
Art Institute, San Antonio; and the Dallas
Museum of Fine Arts, Dallas

Published for the Amon Carter Museum of Western Art
by the
University of Texas Press
Austin and London

The Amon Carter Museum of Western Art was established under the will of the late Amon G. Carter for the study and documentation of westering North America. The program of the Museum is expressed in publications, exhibitions, and permanent collections related to the many aspects of American culture, both historic and contemporary, which find their identification as Western.

Mitchell A. Wilder, Director Amon Carter Museum of Western Art

Library of Congress Catalog Card No. 66-28698 Copyright © 1966 Amon Carter Museum of Western Art All rights reserved Lithographed in USA

ACKNOWLEDGEMENTS

It would not have been possible to write this book about Clara Williamson had she not been so gracious in making herself available to us, and in giving her time whenever it was needed. We wish to thank her for her constant courtesy in permitting us to interview her and to make tape recordings of our conversations together for hours on end; and, during the long planning of this book, for the pleasure of her company.

We give our particular thanks to Mitchell A. Wilder and his staff at Amon Carter Museum for their encouragement and ready assistance whenever needed; to the staff of the University of Texas Press for their careful editing of the manuscript; and to Scott Gentling, whose sensitive and thoughtful portrait study of Aunt Clara has been used for our frontispiece. Our sincere thanks go also to the owners of the Williamson paintings, who have been graciously helpful with information about individual pictures, and in particular to those who have so kindly permitted the reproduction of their paintings for this book.

CONTENTS

ILLUSTRATIONS

BLACK-AND-WHITE PLATES

COLOR PLATES

FOREWORD

It is indeed a rare privilege to honor an artist on the threshold of her ninety-second year with a retrospective exhibition of her paintings. It is an even rarer privilege when that artist is still actively and creatively painting, still sharing with us memories and dreams from the world she knew over fourscore years ago. This unique artist is Clara McDonald Williamson, and this retrospective view of her work not only will re-create for all who see it a pioneer childhood on the West Texas frontier, but will secure her place among the acknowledged masters of Primitive painting.

For she is one of that especially gifted group of painters variously referred to as Primitive, Naive, or Natural, to use the most common labels. She paints what she sees and remembers with simple innocence of vision and untutored hand. She seeks no aesthetic truths, belongs to no school, and understands little of art history or the paintings done by others. She paints because of a deep inner need to express what she feels; she creates spontaneously, with little regard for public applause, and with no knowledge of conventions and limitations of style. Decorative simplicity is in her paintings, to be sure, but also the infinite delight in discovery and the vividness of imagination that raise Mrs. Willamson's work from the quaint and charming to the stature of authentic art. With no hesitation I would place her among the ranks of Rousseau, Bombois, Vivin, Bauchant, Pippin, Hicks, and Kane.

As with most naive painters, Clara Williamson had to wait until well along in life to begin her artistic career. It was only after the death of her husband, when she was already in her late sixties, that she had both the freedom and the leisure to release at last the deeply suppressed desire to "make some beauty." She had little or no formal education; she was raised in the tradition of the rough and hard life of the American frontier; she had no opportunity to break the mold or pattern of her daily work and life. Her friends have been from her neighborhood: the hard-working shopkeepers and small merchants, her neighbors, her relatives and family, her fellow church members.

This environmental pattern is common to naive painters, for the inner world they paint is theirs alone and does not come to them through cultural associations and the study of art and its history. If they visit museums and enjoy the works of art they see there, they are not actually inspired by them; it is rare that such painters find purely cultural events stimulating or even interesting. The restriction of their lives and interests leaves them pure to paint with total honesty their inventions, their memories, their dreams, and even the life around them as they, and they only, experience it. This is the great generosity of the naive painters — that they share this inner life, these personal essences, with us. They paint from the heart, from pure emotion and love; not from the intellectual or the scientific or anything that they have learned or been taught.

When the release came for Clara Williamson, she drew from a full, warm reservoir of memories to guide the hand and brush. There was no gradual evolution of style. With her first expression of one of these memories in a painting her very personal style emerged complete. Her particular genius sets her apart even among the important naive painters. For her pictures have a true atmosphere; air surrounds the objects in them, both animate and inanimate. She captures the clarity of the atmosphere indigenous to the Southwest more successfully than anyone else who has painted it; the clean, clear, soft light that enables one to see objects sharply defined at vast distances is tangible in her paintings. The human beings and animals with which she has peopled her canvases are all alive; they are individuals, known friends, who breathe and talk, walk, dance, run, and jump. They are not brightly hued cardboard cutouts, seemingly pasted on a canvas — they are round and whole and alive and they exist in an atmosphere that can sustain them, of which even the temperature can be felt as it varies from painting to painting. In her landscapes the trees and plants are growing. The subtle, over-all color tonality with which she invests each painting can come only from her instinctive taste and ingenuous vision, as does her remarkable sense of design and incomparably inventive composition.

Wilhelm Uhde, in speaking of Camille Bombois in his book *Five Primitive Masters,* might also have been speaking of Clara Williamson:

"... it is life itself that interests Bombois — the primary energy and endless vitality of life, not secondary or temporary significances. When he paints a path, it leads somewhere. His bridges are substantial bridges; his churches seem to be built of actual brick and stone. His art is not an expression of sensibility via symbolism, but sensibility expressed via delight in literal fact and form.

"The objects he paints are almost literal facts, and take on almost physical form by virtue of his magical sense of the third dimension. One can all but pace off the distance between any two given points in a Bombois scene, or measure the length of a bridge, the width of a footpath, the distance along a winding road. Bombois has become, indeed, one of the great masters of painted depth and space ... there is full, tangible body to whatever Bombois draws, not simply length, breadth and surface. It is once again, life that interests him — life that he can touch, grasp, fondle and embrace."

It is now over twenty years since I first met Aunt Clara. I had gone into one of the classrooms at the Dallas Museum, and after glancing at the still-life setup (an old, well-worn Indian blanket, some Indian corn, and a fine old cooking pot), and the students grouped around it busily endeavoring to reproduce it with some fidelity on their canvases, my attention was caught by an elderly woman, sitting off to herself at an easel bench in a far corner of the room. She was dabbing away with a sable brush on a canvas; her interest far from the Indian still life. She was herself a study in concentration, so engrossed was she in her work. Aunt Clara was painting her first memory picture.

I was drawn to her, so separate from the others, and I smile even now remembering my surprise at what I saw as I stood behind her and watched her procedure in filling her canvas. She was about halfway down, having started painting at the top, and was gradually moving down the canvas, as if lowering a window shade, filling in her penciled outline. Her embarrassment could be felt as she sensed my presence behind her, and my obvious interest in what she was doing. She stopped and turned, and after I had apologized for interrupting her work, and had introduced myself, I couldn't resist asking, "Why do you paint as if pulling a shade?" And she answered, with direct simplicity, "To keep my hands from getting in the paint."

We talked together for some time, and while we chatted, my eyes kept returning to her painting. I was so taken with it that I left her only after securing her promise to sell the picture to me when it was completed. This was *Chicken for Dinner*, the painting that opened the gates of the reservoir to the many memories and dreams that from that day were to flow continually on to her canvases.

At that time I was a young painter, and perhaps more concerned with my own work and its promotion than with that of others, but I was so immediately convinced of the exceptional quality and natural genius inherent in this woman's work that I felt, even then, that it must be shared with others. I had occasion the following year to go to New York on personal business, and, thinking this might be just the opportunity I was seeking to let the world know of Aunt Clara's work, I took with me my own recently acquired *Chicken for Dinner* and two other canvases borrowed from her. I had no business relationship then with Mrs. Williamson, nor even any authority to speak for her; she had given only reluctant and grudging consent that I take her work with me. So I went armed merely with the conviction that this was a talent that must be seen and known where it would be appreciated.

My first visit was to the Museum of Modern Art, which had recently closed a handsome and comprehensive exhibition of Primitive paintings, and more specifically, to Dorothy Miller, curator of painting, who most graciously consented to see and talk with me, and to look at the paintings of my "unknown." She examined them carefully and with evident pleasure, then told me how unfortunate it was that she had not known of Clara Williamson a little earlier, as such an artist not only would have been invited to participate in the exhibition just concluded, but might well have been the star of the show. The visit was very rewarding, and, upon her warm recommendation, I then took the paintings to the Perls Gallery, which already represented several important Primitive painters.

I found Klaus Perls, with his great interest in fine Primitive painting, as receptive and excited by Mrs. Williamson's pictures as Miss

Miller had been, and as generous with his time and enthusiasm. Further, he promptly offered an exhibition to this "unknown," and I promised to convey his offer with its terms and conditions to Mrs. Williamson, since I was not at liberty to speak in her behalf. And this I did upon my return to Dallas. I told Aunt Clara of the fine reception her work had been given, and of the proffered exhibition at the Perls Gallery. But she was unimpressed with my excitement and all that I told her, and against my express advice to do otherwise, refused the exhibition, simply because "it sounds too complicated. I don't know the man, and I don't think I'd better get involved so far away from home."

This decision on her part I have always regretted for her, because, if she had accepted the generous offer made by Klaus Perls, and the subsequent promotion and offers that would surely have followed, her work would now be even better known around the world. I must admit, however, that even without this early promotion which she might have had Clara Williamson is still the best known painter, internationally, living and working in Texas today.

The trip to New York with Aunt Clara's paintings under my arm and my involvement with a museum and a gallery on her behalf because of a belief and a conviction, was the initial cause of a change, a new direction, in my own life. This episode was my initiation into the handling of another artist's work, and it led to a comprehension of the real need of many artists to have an agent or dealer to speak and act for them — to make the decisions regarding placement and other aspects of their finished work. So, in a sense, I owe to Aunt Clara the fact that I am today not only a painter, but also the director of Valley House Gallery.

Our relationship over these many years has been very rewarding to me. I have been an ardent supporter of her painting career since its inception, first as friend, and later as agent and dealer. But primarily I have enjoyed over these twenty-odd years a warm and gradually ripening friendship with this wonderful woman. And for at least the last ten of them I have wanted to do a book about Aunt Clara and her paintings — her life and her legacy in paint. Plans for this retrospective exhibition at the Amon Carter Museum in Fort Worth brought the opportunity for such a book to come into being.

Through this book we can explore at close hand the places and events and persons and things that formed her life, her memories, her paintings. Through the innocent eyes of a child we shall experience the last frontier, the covered wagon, the horse and buggy, the coming of the railroad, arbor prayer meetings, cattle drives, even the automobile and the airplane. We are invited to share with understanding, to participate in the life of a young girl who was gifted with almost total recall, and further gifted with integrity of vision sufficient to enable her to re-create the daily routines and special moments of pleasure.

Missing in her pictures are only disasters, tragedies, and sadness. There has been no time or desire to record such moments, no room for such memories in the rush of the others to be told. We are not even to know, from her paintings, that these elements were present. There is no complaint to be sensed in them; only a humor that never gives way; only refreshment and delight in a past from which she has distilled for us the essence.

Looking over her work and living with it in the preparation of this book, and spending as much time with Aunt Clara as her health and my time would permit, has been an exhilarating and exceptionally rewarding experience. It has been a real privilege, also, to assist in the selection of the paintings for this exhibition. I am confirmed in my certainty that she has a unique place among America's important painters.

As the day grows old, the shadow lengthens; when the light fails, the shadow is usually lost. Aunt Clara has cast a shadow of some length, but when the light is gone, her shadow will grow even longer. It will always be there to remind one of another time; the dreams and life of an era, remembered through the genius and brush of the painter, Clara McDonald Williamson.

Aunt Clara

Aunt Clara was born Clara Irene McDonald, November 20, 1875, in a little Texas frontier town in Bosque County that had only just received its name of Iredell. Her parents had migrated to this small settlement, from their home in Limestone County near Mexia, with other relatives in a wagon train when her brother, a few years her senior, was just a baby. She remembers her mother's account of driving the team and wagon in the train, with the baby on the seat beside her; of having fallen a little behind the others when the little one started crying with hunger, and of the mother's frantic concern and agitation as she drove the team hard to catch up with the others and the chuck wagon, that she might tend her crying child. These were pioneers, and in those early days of growth Bosque County was "West" Texas, peopled sparsely with settlers who wanted more land or a fresh start, or both.

Iredell (named after the first child born there, one Ira Keeler) came into being in a lovely valley on the north side of the Bosque River, not far from where the Duffau flows into the Bosque from the north. The combined streams form a river that may have swelled to flooding some winters, and slowed to a trickle in the summer, but did *not* go dry; so the little settlement prospered, water being the equivalent of gold.

I shall dwell much on Iredell as it was at this period, and as I have learned about it from Aunt Clara's paintings and the many talks we have had about it together. For as she says, "Of course now, that was my world; that was all I knew, that little town, and of course that's all I had to remember and put on canvas, and I think a painter ought to paint what he knows like an author ought to write what *he* knows."

And at the time that Aunt Clara best remembers her little world and shares it with us in her paintings, Iredell could boast a population of around eight hundred, and a main street (McClain Street) bordered by a train depot, a carpenter shop, a saloon, a hotel, a combined dry-goods/hardware store, and a few other such necessary business establishments. The community supported two churches, Baptist and Methodist (which doubled on weekdays as schools), and a communal cemetery. The town was made up of "good Christian people," to quote Aunt Clara, "preachers, farmers, teachers and all — but it was a mixed bag, too," and included a few criminals and "an occasional dealing with carpetbaggers who came down from the North." For periodic excitement there were the cattle drives and the cowboys, as Iredell was a stopover on the Old Chisholm Trail from the south to Kansas City; and the occasional Indian raids that usually cost a fat steer or a favorite horse and brought the special feeling of danger. But in general the people were stable — good people who worked hard to maintain life and family, and passed to their children a great sense of moral courage and responsibility.

Her father, Thomas McDonald, was a prime example of this character, but his background was spiced with a particular aura of excitement. Orphaned by the death of both parents during the Civil War, young Tom and his even younger brother, John, who was around seven or eight, by the end of the war, had been indentured to a farmer in Collin County for farm work. His older brother, Alexander, returned home from the war wounded, "with a bullet lodged in his spine," but evidently still very capable and determined to care for his little brothers. When he discovered what had occurred, he waited until nightfall, then "stole them away in the bitter cold." He wrapped them both in blankets, set them on a horse, and headed them north with himself in the lead, turning occasionally to hit them with his quirt when they threatened to fall asleep and hence off the horse. Since this event occurred in a blizzard and saved the boys from a life of bondage, it makes a vivid picture and a dramatic story. The wounded elder brother, besides his great sense of family responsibility, had an equally great sense of family honor, and is credited with having paid off any claims made against his father after the War, even though he felt many of them were false and unjust. This was the heritage of Tom McDonald, and one he did not hesitate to instill in his children.

He was by profession a millwright and carpenter, although his brothers turned to farming and Aunt Clara speaks of her cousins "running cattle." The only carpenter in the territory, he was kept constantly occupied, building everything from the "flouring-mill on the south side of the river for Mr. Carter" to the refined frame houses that followed the log houses of the settlers; from the furniture for their homes and washbenches and tubs, to the coffins that were their last resting places.

Her mother's antecedents, although not perhaps as dashing, were equally solid. Mary Lasswell came from the Kentucky Lasswells, but she herself was a native Texan, born in Limestone County. Her father was an imposing man, standing six-feet-six in his stocking feet, and his superior height assured him of a position of authority wherever he might be. He was a part of the family migration to Bosque County, and lived with his daughter and her family during most of Clara's childhood. Mary Lasswell McDonald was a handsome woman, with dark eyes and hair and a serene composure unshaken by life as a frontier wife and mother. She produced six children over a period of almost twenty years, the first arriving when she was nineteen, and the last when she was almost forty. The second of these was Clara, the only child in the family to favor her father in coloring, being blue-eyed, and variously referred to as "tow-headed" or "sorrel-topped." Aunt Clara says often of her brothers and sisters, "Every one of the children was as fine-lookin' — but I was an ornery-lookin' runt." This notion of hers, which she expressed often to me in various ways seemed to stem partly from the fact that she weighed less than five pounds at birth and largely from her admiration of the dark beauty of her mother, and hence of the other children in the family who looked like Mama.

It was a hard and busy life for the women, who had little time for foolishness; their leisure activities usually centered around the church, which provided often only a stern form of amusement. When Clara was born her mother was still spinning thread from cotton of which to weave cloth or to knit their garments. The stores had not yet been built, and everything that came to Iredell came by wagon train; so it was an economy based on raising from or on the earth what one wore as well as what one ate. The women married young, had their first babies promptly, worked hard all their lives, aged rapidly, died young. But Clara remembers her mother as being "as artistic as she could be," for somehow, when Clara was still a baby, Mary McDonald found the minutes in which to paint a picture (framed by the father), that was "always around." She also hooked rugs, pieced quilts, made the clothes they wore, all from her own designs, and, according to her loving daughter, all beautiful and "artistic." The very romantic view Clara held for her mother in no way belied the firm, quiet, no-nonsense strictness with which this wise woman raised her family.

The land to which the McDonalds came was "the prettiest place you ever saw, but life was hard and sad." It was post-oak country, and before the fertile land could be cultivated the tough post-oaks must be

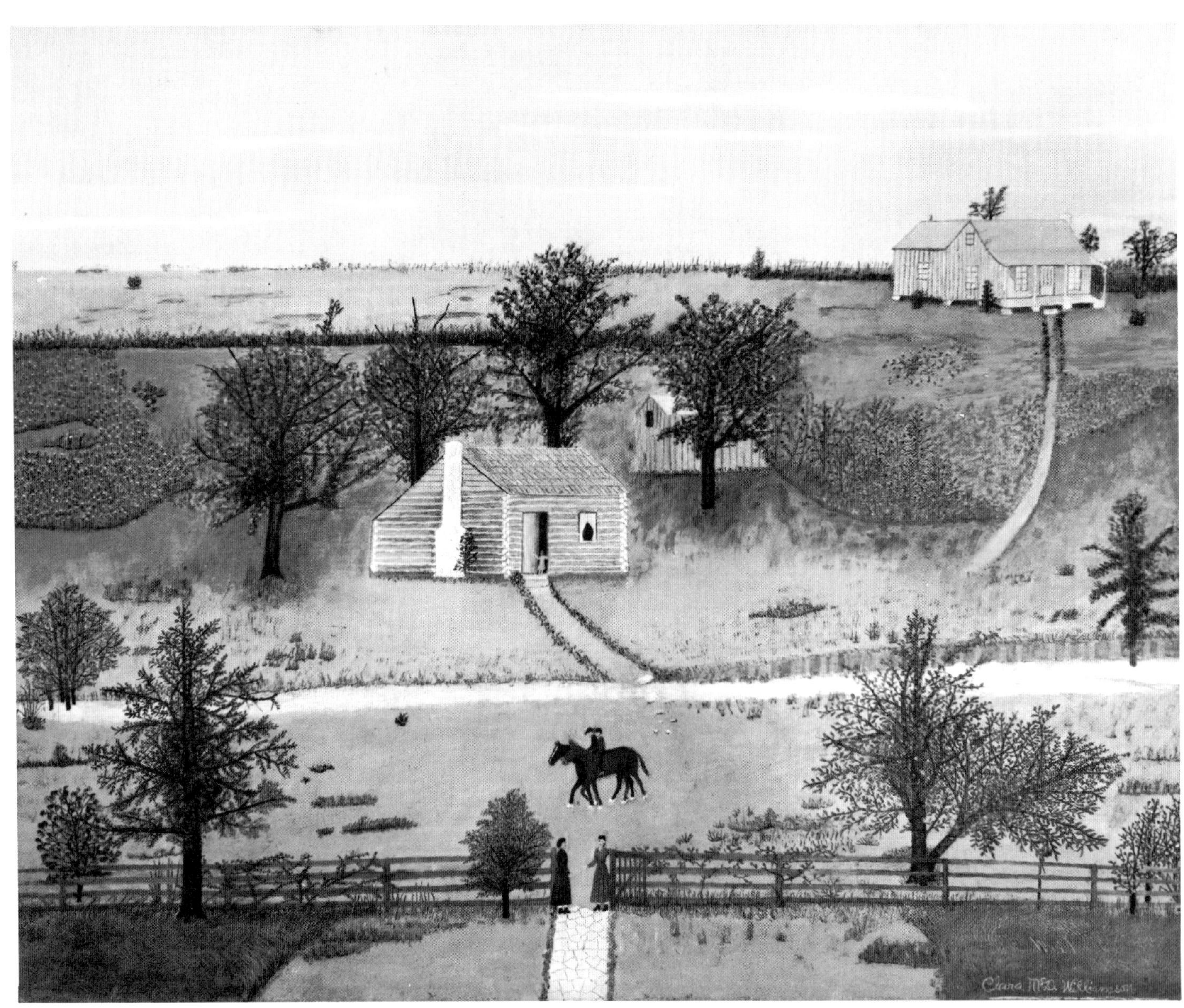

MY BIRTHPLACE
Oil on canvas, 1966, 24 x 30 in.; courtesy Dr. and Mrs. P. M. Williamson, Dayton, Ohio

cleared and cabins built to house the burgeoning families. But in this particular the McDonalds were fortunate, as they came across an abandoned log cabin shortly after their arrival at the settlement, and moved right in. Many of these empty cabins were scattered around that country, abandoned by those who found the Indian raids too harassing, or the life of the frontier too hard, or by those who could not rest without another push to the West. The cabin found by the McDonalds provided an immediate shelter and temporary quarters that served them well while Tom McDonald waited for new lumber to come by ox train from Waco, and then longer, while he built a fine frame house for his family, and a carpenter shop for himself just down the street.

Clara was born in this cabin and lived there for almost three years before they moved into the frame house across the street. And in her ninety-first year she has completed a canvas (slightly above her average size) of this cabin in which she was born, which she simply calls, *My Birthplace*. The cabin dominates the center of the picture, while directly down from it is the path leading to the new home, with her mother in violet standing talking to a cousin who has in her turn moved into the cabin. The child peering out of the door of the cabin is the cousin's child, the young men on horseback trotting down the street "are just boys, I think they may be the Phillips boys who lived just down the way there." The street was the main street of Iredell, McClain Street, which her father's new shop also faced. The house to the upper right was built of boxing lumber (a scornful term, indeed). The water flowing beside the street in the dranage ditch is from a spring shower that just washed the dust from air and objects and left the atmosphere clear and fresh. The sky itself is clear and transparent, and has been given a feeling of movement. The horizontal lines of the fence, ditch, hedgerow, horizon and the long thin floating clouds, all broken in turn by the vertical thrust of trees and paths, create a most effective spatial division. The clarity of the light is not the result of chance or accident; Aunt Clara creates her atmospheres with a hand guided by her inner vision. The buildings, although imperfect in linear perspective, are instinctively sure in their outlines, and are beautiful in surface quality. They work perfectly in forming related spatial areas that lock the composition into an integrated design.

One of our best views of the interior of this cabin is in her painting

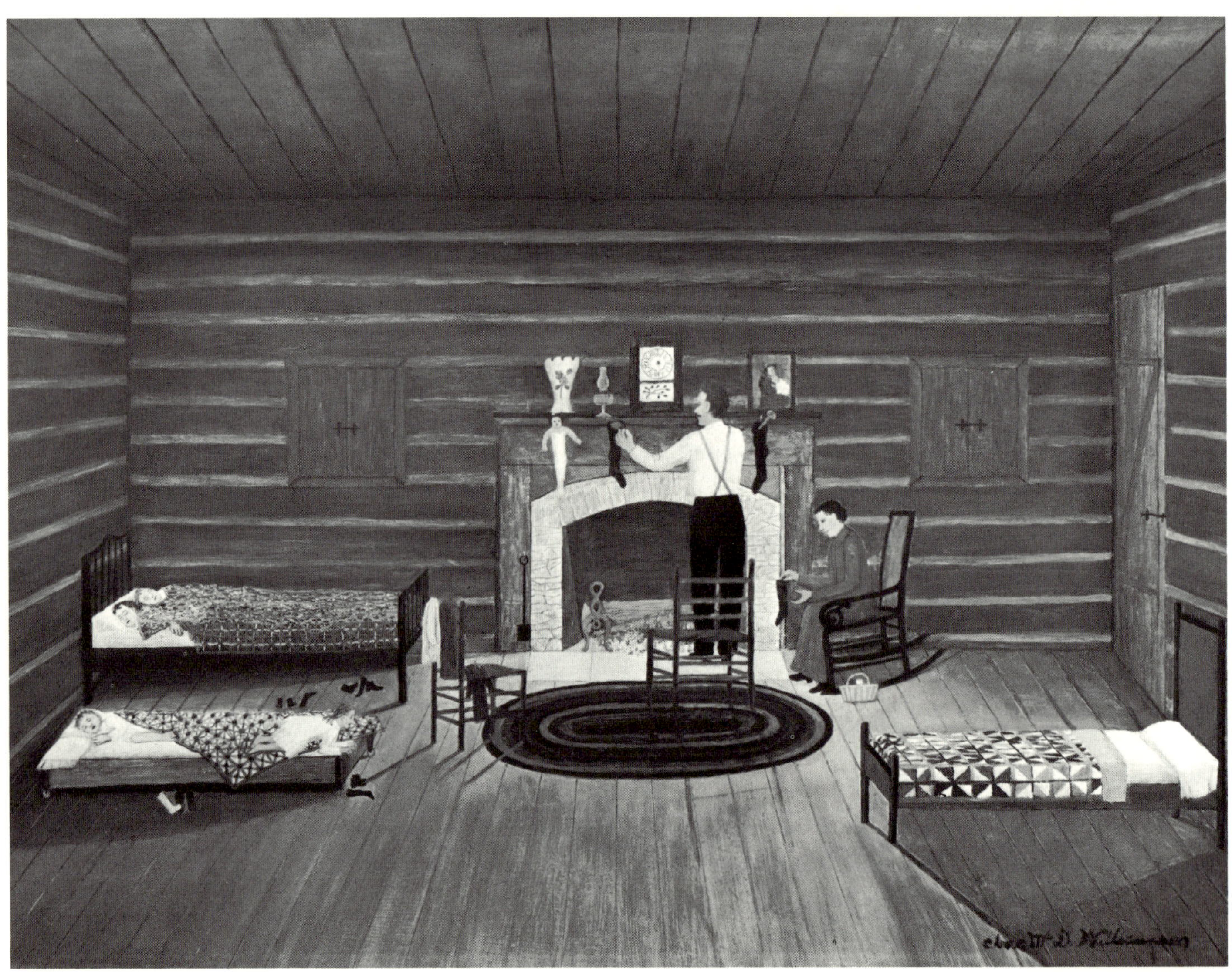

THE NIGHT BEFORE CHRISTMAS
Oil on panel, 1954, 18 x 24 in.; courtesy Miss Suzanne Simmons, Dallas

of *The Night before Christmas,* which shows the one big room of the cabin with its center of family life, the fireplace. The lean-to on the outside provided the only other room, although it was often divided in two, permitting the settler to speak of his cabin as having "three rooms." In this painting Clara shares with us one of her earliest memories, that of staying awake on Christmas Eve in the trundle bed in which she slept with her baby sister, and hoping to see Santa Claus come down the chimney. She speaks of creeping out from under the covers and hiding behind a chair, and of seeing, instead of Santa Claus, her mother and father filling the stockings that had been hung at the mantel. When I asked her what she found the next morning in her stocking she said that usually each child received an apple, an orange, and a bit of candy, and perhaps a cheap doll. I indicated my surprise that there were no toys made by her father and mother, and she told me with asperity that they didn't have time to make toys.

They also had little time or inclination to coddle their children. Her father demonstrated little affection for Clara, and since, as she says, he very seldom noticed her, she was "on top of the world when Father would pay some attention to me." And one memory that she has not recorded in paint, and that predates even the Christmas Eve on which she awaited Santa Claus to no avail, was such a moment with her father.

It was a bright Sunday afternoon when she was still small enough to be carried. Her father had hitched the horse to the hack, and she and her mother and father and beloved older brother had all taken a drive to Johnson's Peak. It was such a fine afternoon that they decided to climb the peak, no mean feat in Sunday finery. It was a hard climb, and in many places one almost had to crawl, using the brush just ahead as a handle in achieving the next step up. The triumph and delight of this memory was that her father picked Clara up in his arms, and carried her all the way to the crest of the peak, leading the way for the struggling and laughing mother and brother to follow. She can still look back over his shoulder to watch the others as he laughs in her ear and says, "Look at that! They can't walk up the mountain — they can only crawl!" She was so full of happiness this day that she even remembers and describes with exactness just how the huge rock capping the peak looked, cracked in half as it was by some primal movement of the earth.

During these days when the first children were too small to take their later chores, the father did help from time to time with the mother's work. On Sundays (a well-cherished day, with everyone at home) he would sit in a back room of the new frame house and churn for her mother. From this position he could look to the north and a high hill overlooking the settlement and the river, and all the while he churned, he would stare at the hill, and dream of building a house there, in the grove of native pecan trees that topped its height.

When the railroad started moving towards Iredell, and the crews came in to survey for the track and depot, they also surveyed the surrounding land and laid it out in lots. Tom McDonald was one of the first on hand to put his name down to make certain the lot on top of the hill was his — the highest land around. Here he could build a house to be proud of, facing south to gather the strong summer breeze and protected from the chilling northers by a second small rise on the crest of the hill that would lie behind the house.

And while he dreamed and planned his house on the hill, the railroad tracks and the train itself arrived in Iredell. Aunt Clara has recorded this for us in one of her most exciting paintings, *The Building of the Railroad*. She was almost five, and the men working on the track had let out word that the locomotive itself was on its way. So, chores being done, everyone who could go hurried to the track to see the train come in. Clara is the little girl in the blue dress; her baby sister, Addie, is being carried in her mother's arms, and at this moment Clara has just said, "I'm not afraid of that big iron thing," when the whistle blew and the steam hissed — "and I was, oh, so scared, and I grabbed Mama's skirt, and, oh, just hid!" It can readily be seen that she felt others were as frightened by the black monster as she was, for she shows the wagon horses bolting in such frenzy that a small girl is thrown from the wagon, her hat cartwheeling into the sky as her father tries to stop the runaways. The deer in the high pasture are seen running wildly in terror — only the teams of plow mules and the stolid men laying the track are unaffected by the excitement and novelty of this great adventure.

In painting this experience, so stimulating to her as a child, Aunt Clara has also pictorialized a capsule history of railroad building in the 1880's. She shows how the train ran right to the end of the tracks as it was needed to bring more ties, track, and supplies for the crew; how the men who laid the track made camp with their chuck-wagon and tents, and moved each day to the end of the line, where they set

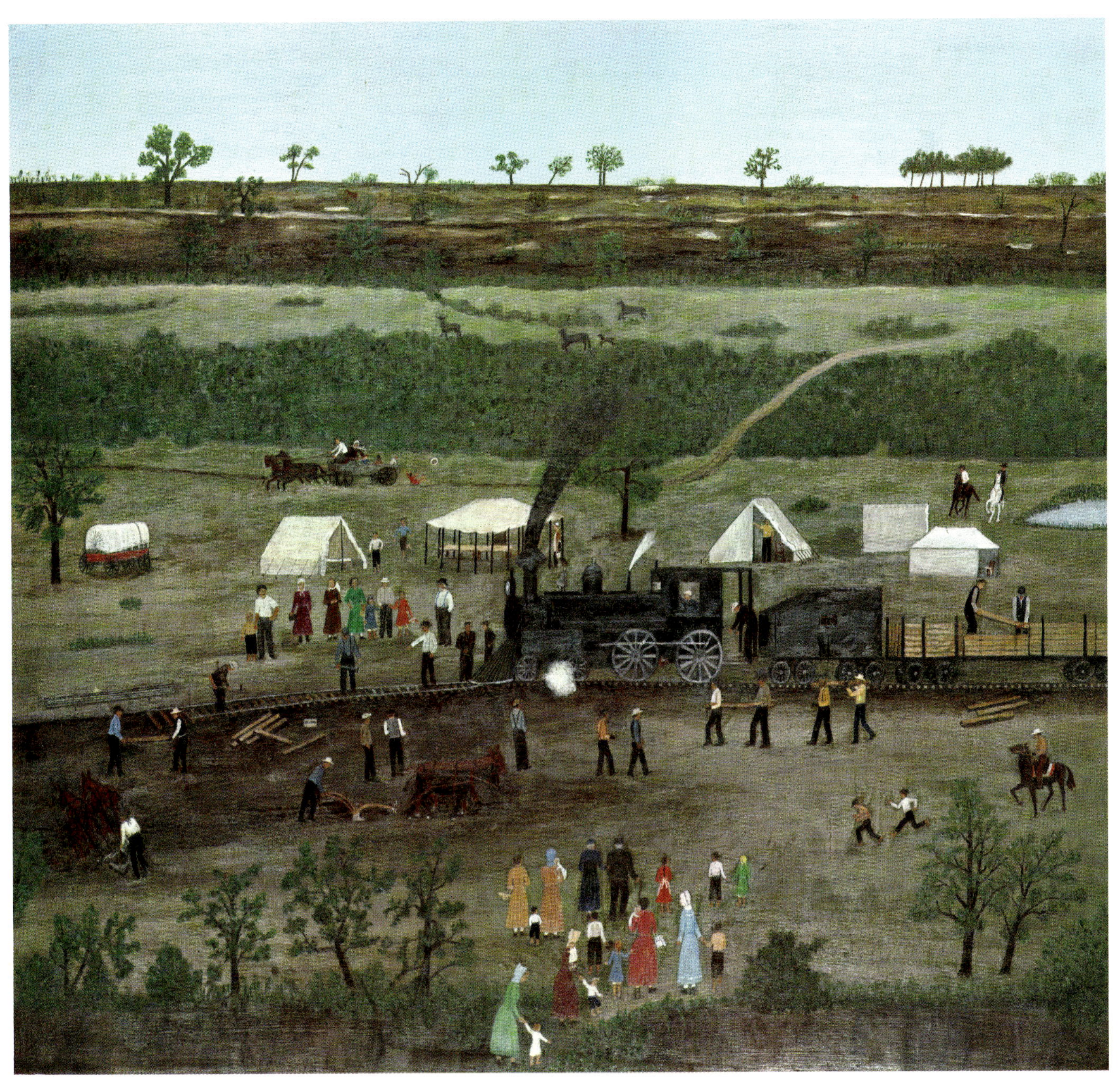

THE BUILDING OF THE RAILROAD
Oil on panel, 1949-1950, 27 x 29½ in.; courtesy Mr. and Mrs. Edward Douglas Cobb, Dallas

up quarters for the night. This is a real train, the crew is really laying track — the children are running, the horses are actually bolting in terror — one can almost hear the comments that pass from one settler to another, and the orders the straw boss gives to his men. This is a part of the genius of Clara Williamson: there is air in her paintings, and through this air her family and friends and others really move and speak and live, as they did for her long ago.

When Clara was almost six, and her baby sister, Addie, was just a year old, preparations were at last made to move into the house on the hill. Her father had spent as much time as he could spare from his other carpenter work in building the fine frame house as he had dreamed it, and now it was completed. The family was delighted, as the house on McClain Street had been sold some months earlier, and they had been living temporarily in the carpenter shop until the new house was ready.

When the wagon had been filled with the last load of goods to be taken up the hill, Clara climbed into the back over the tail gate, and held the baby for the ride to their new home. Aunt Clara remembers this day particularly well, for as they went into the house for the first time, her mother, who had lifted the baby out of the wagon and was carrying her, set her down on the floor for Clara to look after while the wagon was being unloaded. And as Addie's feet touched the floor, she started walking across the room! "Oh, Mama, look! The baby's a'walkin'!" It was Addie's first birthday and they hadn't known she was ready to walk. This little moment made the strange new house immediately a home.

Clara and the other children were kept busy. This was a society in which everyone had to work, even the very little boys and girls. From the time she was born her older brother, Allen, took care of her, and because of this she looked up to him in all things. She also tried to do everything that he did, and when very tiny was an expert runner and tree climber and was generally a tomboy. She was ready for anything he had to suggest, and he enjoyed her companionship while protecting her from "varmints, and such things as wild cattle and bulls." When Adaline was born, Clara in her turn become the guardian and protector, and her freedom and childhood were over. As she put it one day when we were talking about frontier children, "Well, I just went from babyhood right to service." There were no servants in Iredell, partially because no Negroes were permitted to settle in the community when she was a child, and there were no female relatives living with the family who might ease the burden of work for her mother. So, as Clara was the oldest daughter, she was pressed by necessity into service as soon as she was capable of helping.

One of the chores that combined fun and excitement with duty was the important task of catching a chicken for Mama when she wanted to fry one for their dinner. This is recorded in Aunt Clara's first, and certainly most important, memory picture. *Chicken for Dinner* reveals the whole marvelous panorama of Iredell and the Bosque River valley as far as one could see from the house on the hill clear to where a spur of the Davis Mountains touched the horizon and formed the southern boundary of the world. This is where Clara lived uninterruptedly from early childhood until she was in her twenties, and from the eminence of the McDonald Place she watched Iredell grow and change; from this vantage point she saw and learned everything that went on in her world. For surely, with everything she knew spread out in front of her for daily feasting, it was *her* world. And it was a family joke, but true, that she never forgot anything she saw or heard.

The foreground of *Chicken for Dinner* tells the story of the chicken chase. Clara is the blonde child in blue, running hard after the chickens; her sister Addie is in pink, holding out her skirt ("I put Addie in pink because she was such a pretty thing with her huge grey eyes and dark hair") and brother Allen has almost caught the black hen. To the left we see the rear of her home; below this, Uncle Joe, her bachelor uncle who lived with them most of the time, doing the plowing. Behind the children is a young orchard of peach trees, and to the right, the barn, with Prince, her grandfather's blooded saddle horse, sunning himself. ("Grandfather always kept a beautiful saddle horse in that barn. He was so tall and handsome on that horse when he'd go riding by, he looked like a militia man, which he wasn't.") This was the only farm her father bothered with, this bit behind the house. Her mother used a portion of it to keep a good vegetable garden going, staggering her plantings so that the family enjoyed fresh vegetables throughout the season for each, with an abundance to "lay by" for the rest of the year.

A fair piece of land stretches in front of the house before the hill drops to the valley, and, hidden from view by this land and by the height of the hill, is the town of Iredell and the railroad. We see only the roof of one of the buildings in the town itself, then the road to the river and the churches and homes that grew on the south side of the river. Except for the town itself, nearly everything Aunt Clara later reveals to us of her childhood memories comes from this painting. I have mentioned elsewhere that this painting is the key to nearly all the rest, and this is true in every possible way.

She speaks often of her problems in painting it, her troubles with perspective, and in particular with the rock fence that divides the orchard from the pasture behind the barn. "I just couldn't make that rock fence stand up — the teacher wouldn't help me a bit — I warted him to death over this —"

And her handling of perspective in this painting is indeed arbitrary and free. For there are three points of perspective in *Chicken for Dinner*. The relationship of objects in space has been worked out from three different points of reference, a pattern which creates a very effective division of space in a series of diagonals. The stone and wooden fences on either side of the orchard not only divide the areas of the picture in a most interesting way, but also set up a spatial relationship both satisfying and logical. This illustrates primarily her remarkable sense of design and inventiveness.

This personal handling of perspective, which enables her to make a complete statement with the landscape and at the same time to hold the spatial elements firmly together; her sense of space division; and her feeling for the proper relationship between color areas — these qualities place Aunt Clara securely among the most authentic and important masters of naive painting.

Another of Clara's chores, almost as pleasurable as catching the chickens in a rough-and-tumble with the other children in the family, was fetching the water for daily use from the natural artesian spring

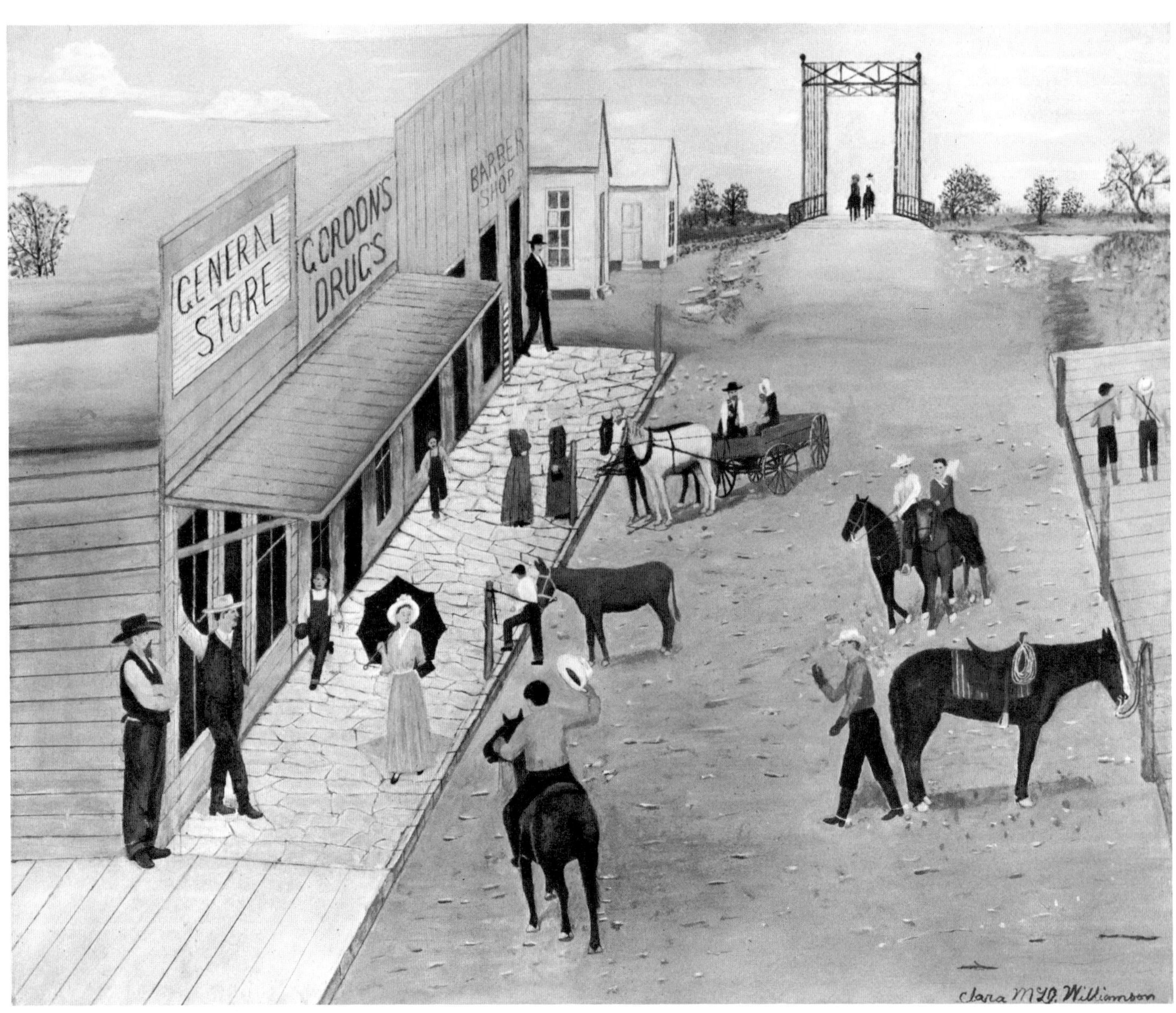

MAIN STREET, IREDELL
Oil on panel, 1950-1951, 20 x 24 in.; courtesy Mr. and Mrs. Howell Smith, Dallas

in the center of the town. Before the wells were dug everyone took water from this spring, and Clara grew even more fleet-footed and strong as she made the many trips, mostly running, down the hill to the town for water, and back up again, arriving home not even out of breath. The pleasures of dawdling in the town can be judged by her paintings, *Main Street, Iredell* and *Sunday Train*. In the first we see the enticement of the newly built stores with their shelves full of the increasingly varied goods brought in from Waco via the railroad. The new dry-goods store, Harris & Sellers, now handled piece goods, marbles, dolls, and even such luxuries as croquet sets. Aunt Clara mentions wryly that her mother had knitted all their stockings until the stores finally got some in, "but when they did, the stockings were *all* black!"

Clara being a child who noticed, we also see a flapper, mincing her way down the walk, flirting with her parasol. We taste the dust in the air, from the sandy, reddish soil of the main street, and feel the heat of the summer day.

Sunday Train introduces us to one of the innocent pleasures of the young people and the families in that time when sources of entertainment were so few. Since only the minimum of work was done on a Sunday, it being forbidden by the Holy Book, the families were free to indulge, on a Sunday afternoon, in the pastime of strolling into town and watching the afternoon train in and out of the depot.

Two passenger trains a day went through Iredell: in the morning, a train from Waco went west, and in the afternoon, around 2:30, it or another returned to the east. But usually, everyone was much too busy to watch the train come in, so on Sundays this was an event to be enjoyed. It was considered quite proper that this occasion be used for a bit of courting, and the young men rode their horses to the station to show off for the young ladies, who either gathered in giggling groups, or walked in pairs down the board walk, with only a sidelong glance at the dashing boys. Only the very daring among the girls would walk alone.

For the married couples it was a further chance to chat and gossip, for often the rush home after church to fix the midday meal precluded any socializing. And for the children it was a time of freedom and pleasure. This is the reason, as with most of her memory pictures, that Aunt Clara has "recorded it" for us. She says of the town, "Iredell was the prettiest town you ever saw before the flood — but

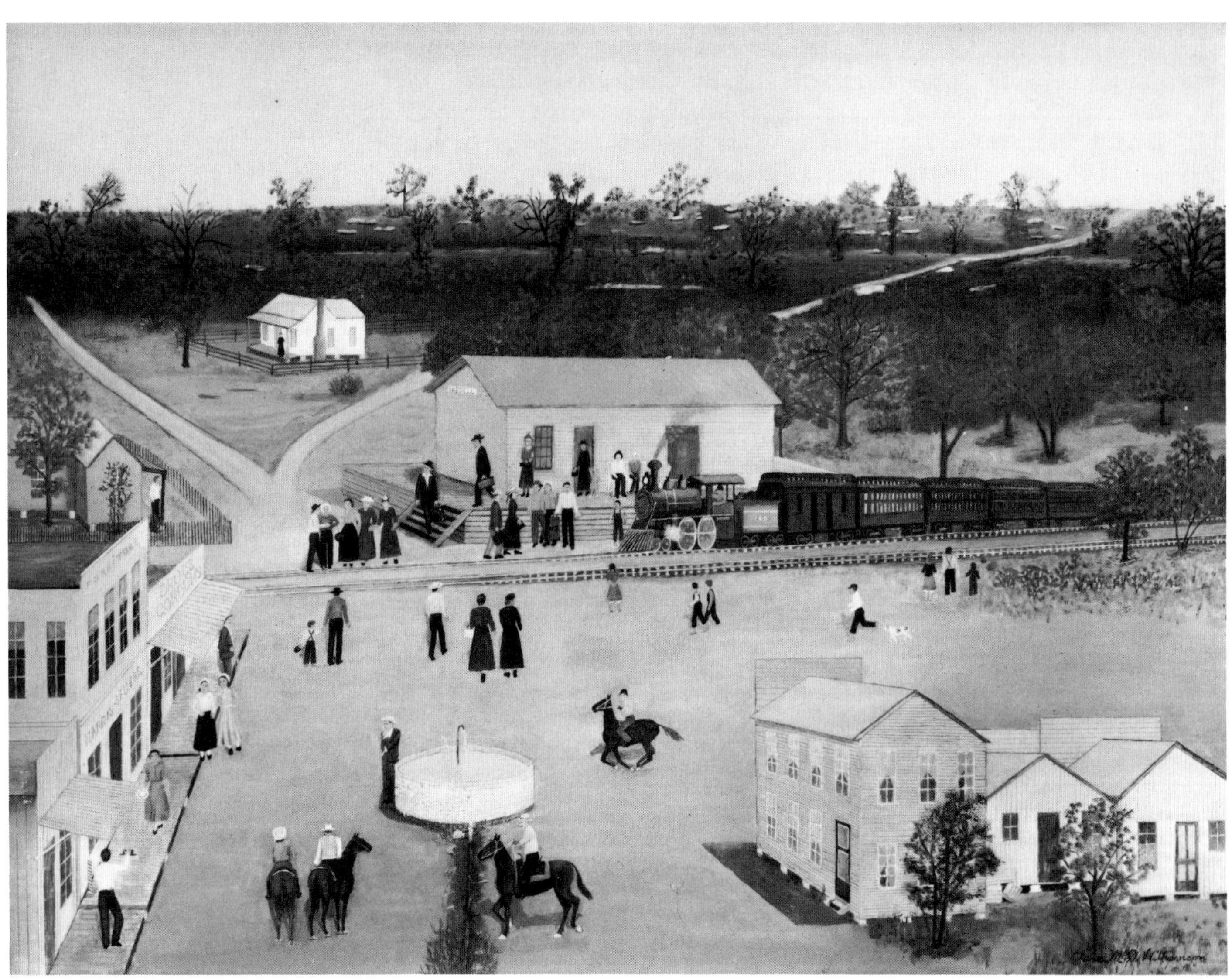

SUNDAY TRAIN
Oil on panel, 1953, 24 x 32 in.; courtesy Robert T. Vanderbilt, Gstaad, Switzerland

things weren't easy — People had a good sense of humor, though, and *some* good things happened." Meeting the Sunday train was undoubtedly one of these.

The two-story building in the right foreground of *Sunday Train* is the Abbott Hotel, and this was the center of transient gaiety in Iredell as well as a pleasure spot for the lighter-minded townsfolk. Here the cowboys with money in their pockets would stay when the cattle drives stopped for the night near Iredell; here the travelers would stop over if their business in Iredell lasted too long to catch the afternoon train back to Waco, or if they were too weary to head farther west on the early morning train.

It was also a meeting place for special parties, and in her *Square Dance* Aunt Clara shows us the dining room of the hotel, which, as it was the largest room, was the one used for balls. There were musicians in Iredell, but for such special dances the music was often imported from Waco — "just a straight run on the railroad." She painted this set of four couples because when she saw them dancing in like manner when she was very small, she thought they "looked kind of funny stepping high like that." It is interesting to note that, although the gentlemen removed their hats before inviting the ladies to join them in the "square," only one found it necessary to also remove his spurs! And the cowboy engaging in light conversation with the lady to the left of the picture has kept on both hat and gun, although his spurs have mysteriously vanished.

In the lower left foreground of *Sunday Train,* next to the young man tipping his hat, is the striped barber pole that gives warning that this is man's territory, and no woman's land. As Aunt Clara told me, "I was always nosing around and seeing things I shouldn't see — you know if a girl passed by a barber shop and looked in, she was considered very forward and bold and disgraced. But *I* peeped in, and no one noticed."

Which is most fortunate, or we should have missed one of her more delightful paintings, *Sweet Adeline.* She evidently peeped in often enough to make quite certain of the members of the barbershop quartet, the most important of whom is the "big, fat fellow with the moustache, Bill Buchanan — he had a great voice; if trained, he would have made an opera singer." The very distinguished gentleman waiting his turn by the mirrored hat rack is Dr. Marvin Grace, who took care of Clara when she nearly died of typhoid fever at the

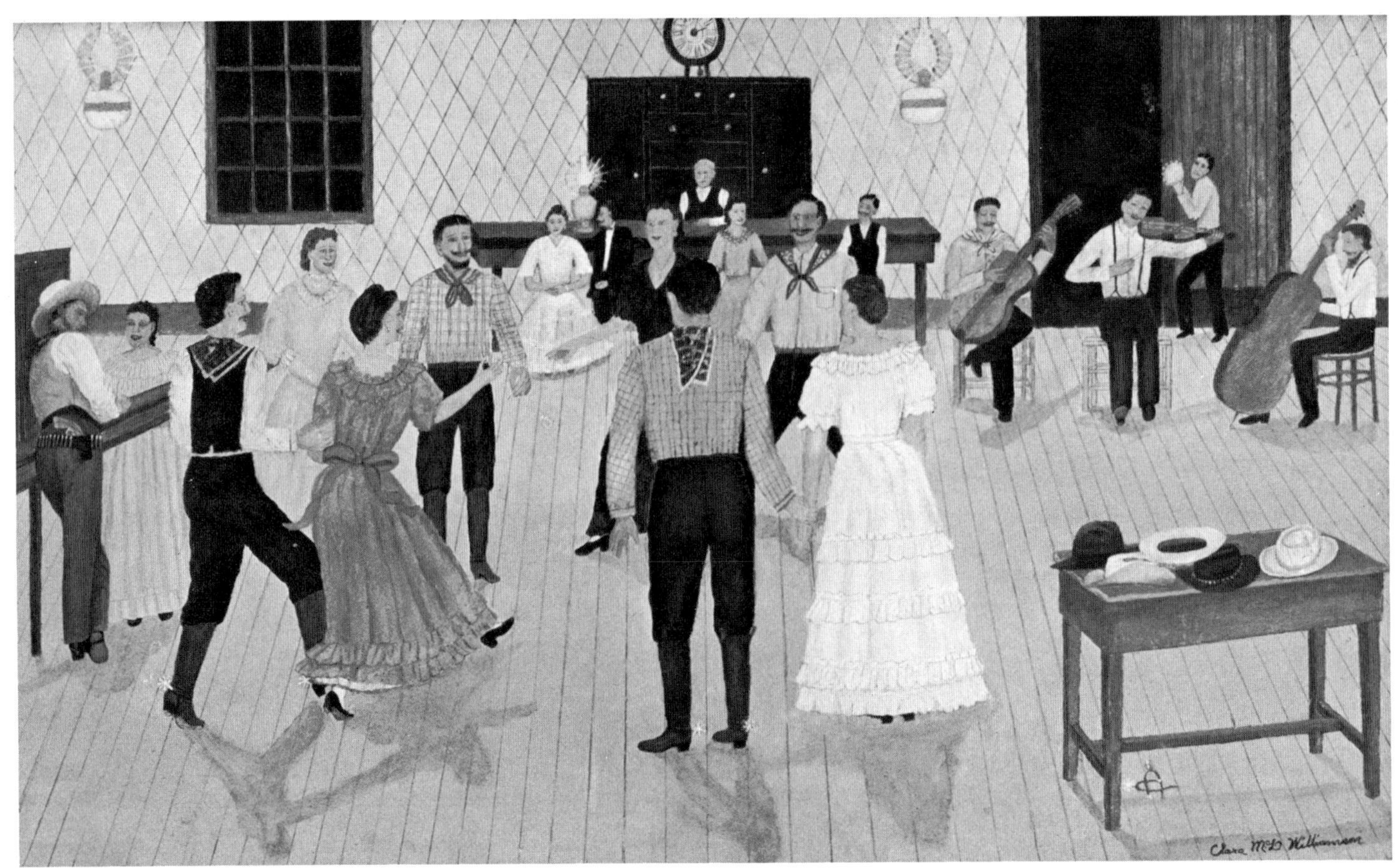

SQUARE DANCE
Oil on panel, 1955, 15 x 25 in.; courtesy Valley House Gallery, Dallas

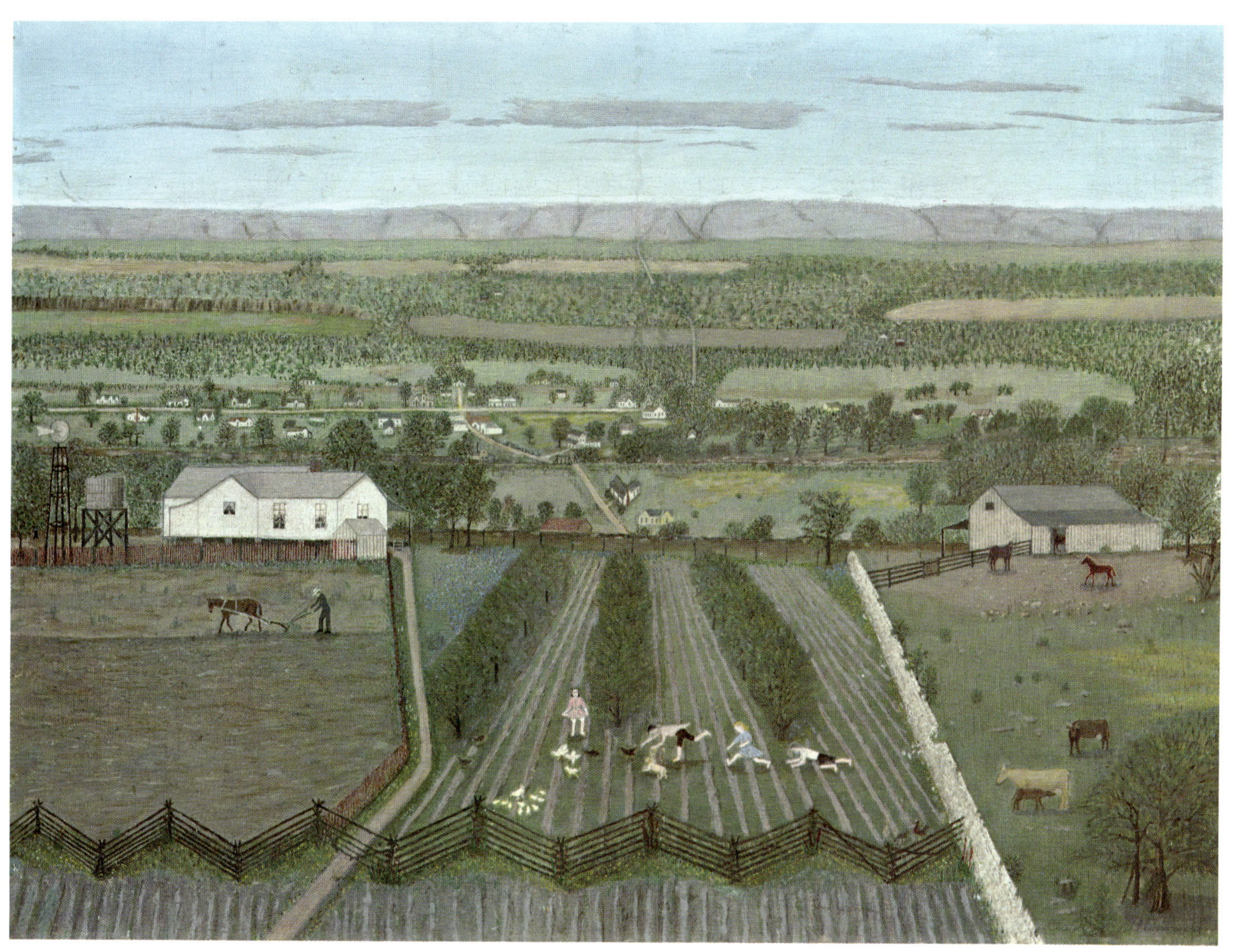

CHICKEN FOR DINNER
Oil on canvas, 1945, 22½ x 30¼ in.; courtesy Mr. and Mrs. Donald F. Vogel, Dallas

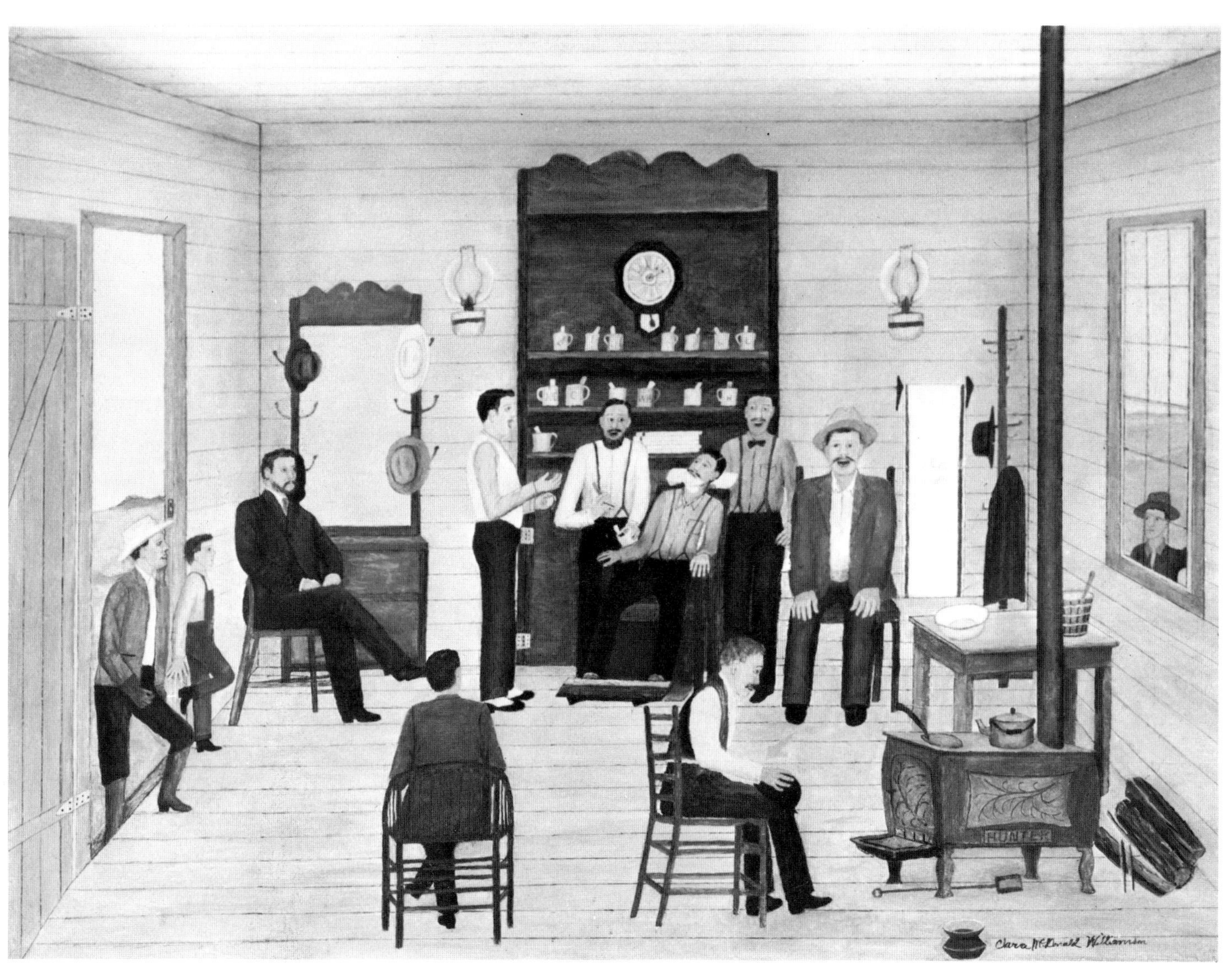

SWEET ADELINE
Oil on panel, 1955, 18 x 24 in.; courtesy Mr. and Mrs. Thomas N. Overton, Dallas

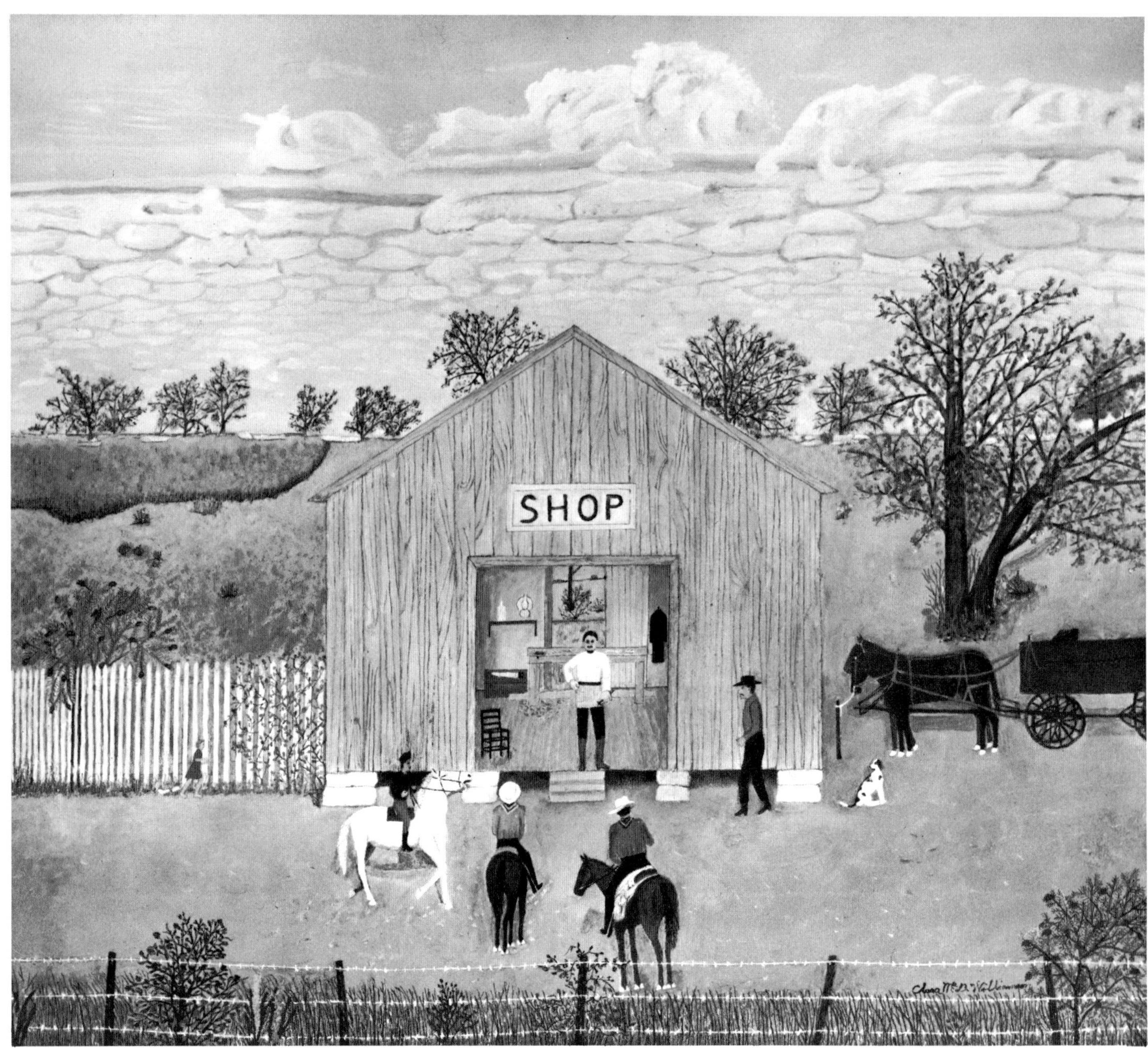

FRONTIER CARPENTER SHOP
Oil on canvas, 1965, 26 x 30 in.; courtesy Valley House Gallery, Dallas

age of eighteen. There was always plenty of wood to keep the black stove hot and welcoming, and the water steaming; the roller towel was always dirty, as it was just rolled over and over and rarely changed; the mugs on the shelves were kept ready to provide the means for a clean shave in a relaxed and totally male atmosphere.

Her father's place of business was another haven that attracted the men of the village (along with Clara), and she has painted it as it must have looked when she and her family lived in the frame house just down the street. She calls it *Frontier Carpenter Shop,* and shows her father taking a breather as he welcomes some friends who have stopped by for business and a chat. The shop was very poorly equipped in the earliest days: it boasted a few saws, some knives (in particular a knife known as a Barlow knife), axes, and hunting knives. And when Tom McDonald first set up in business in Iredell he had no nails — only wooden pegs that he made himself. Later, when the ox trains started coming in regularly from Waco, and then the railroad, his equipment and tools became more refined. The shop was always exceptionally orderly, and the tools were kept sharp and in near-perfect condition.

As noted earlier, Tom McDonald was the coffin maker for the countryside. The coffins were simple rectangular boxes, built to size with screw-down lids, but they were decorated quite beautifully inside with lace all around the inner edge and with the finest cotton or linen available lining the interior. It was while Tom was finishing one of these coffins that Jim Terrell, the gambler, came by one afternoon, much in the manner of the men on horseback in front of the shop in the painting.

"What are you doing, Tom?" asked the gambler.

"Oh, I'm making a resting place for some soul down the way."

"What do you want to be wasting your time at doing that for, Tom?"

"You'd better be careful the next one's not for you, Jim!"

And as Aunt Clara puts it, it was only three weeks later that Terrell was killed by a man named Sneed, another gambler. They had been gambling down in the creek bottoms, and one decided that the other was cheating, and "they got in a fuss. Well, Sneed just killed Jim Terrell, and left him there, and when his family hunted for him there on the island where the water goes around — when they found him, the wild hogs had eaten his face, you know. Sneed went off on foot

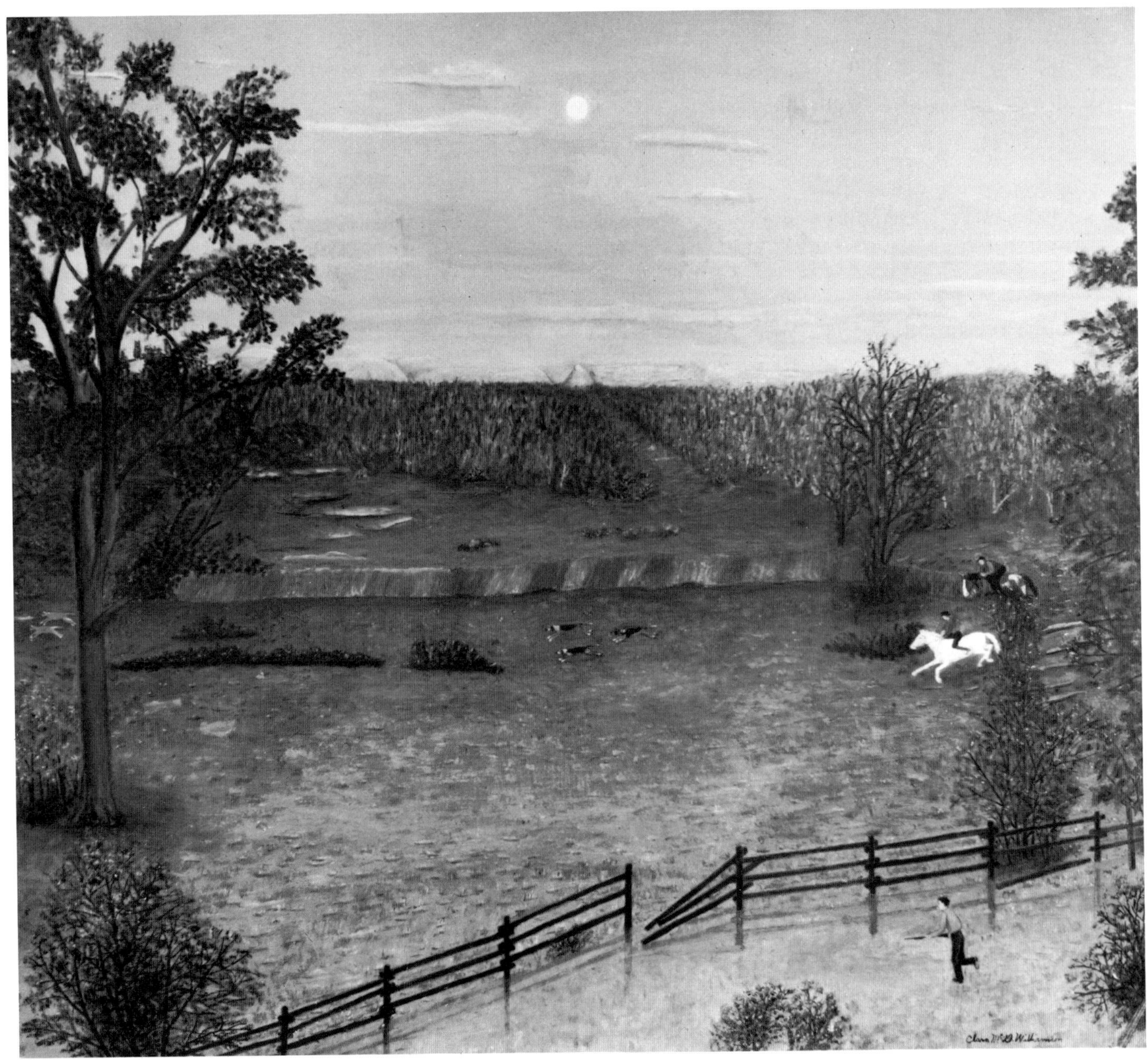

THE NIGHT HUNTERS
Oil on panel, 1955-1956, 24 x 27 in.; courtesy Robert W. Decherd, Dallas

and someone saw him wash his hands and face in the river — and no one saw him from that time to eternity! Will Terrell, Jim's small son, swore he'd hunt him up and kill him, and of course, he never saw him — now that's frontier Texas for you!"

And Tom made the coffin for gambler Jim Terrell, who left a poor pregnant wife and four children when Sneed shot him.

*　　*　　*

The nights in Iredell held their own special beauty and enchantment. A part of this is captured in *The Night Hunters* and in the story about it that Aunt Clara wrote for the University of Illinois Catalogue in 1952, the painting having been included in the exhibition of that year:

"My childhood home was on a high hill overlooking to the south, a beautiful valley along the little Bosque River, with a spur of the Davis Mountains to be seen far to the south. With the changing seasons of the year, this made an interesting and beautiful scene; especially on a still, bright moon-lit night; then the view was enchanting.

"In this section of Texas, at that time, the scattered settlers were plagued by wild-cats, coyotes (or wolves) killing their calves, lambs and poultry. Some farmers and ranchers kept several fine-blooded and trained hound dogs, for the protection of their property. The hunters would meet at a decided place and assemble their dogs by blowing their horn (which would be made from a cow's horn). Then the horse-back riders would ride with the delighted dogs in the lead. They would gain reinforcements and momentum as other men and boys would join the race, both on foot and horse-back, as the hunters passèd their way. Often they would hunt until the wee hours of the morning.

"When a child, I would be awakened from a sound sleep, on my little trundle bed, by the hunters' 'Hi Hi Sicum' (a good old Texas word, but I guess it's not English) urging the yelping hounds on in the distance. I would become very excited and would usually pull the cover over my head and scrounge down in my bed, but on one, this, occasion, I became so interested that I jumped from my bed and ran barefooted to the brink of the hill. And this is what I saw and tried to tell in my painting *Night Hunters*."

Sundays in Iredell were primarily dedicated to more serious gatherings than that of meeting the Sunday train at the depot in town. There was, when possible, the weekly reinforcement of Christian principle and mores by regular attendance at church, and Clara's mother saw to it that all of her children were thus reinforced from the time they were born. This involved an adventurous route to church from the house on the hill; first down the hill and across the valley to the river, then across the river to the south bank, and then to church. If the decision was to walk instead of going by horse and buggy and fording the river, one could still either choose to go across on stepping stones, or take the ferry, which was simply a small rowboat.

Both churches, the Baptist and the Methodist, were on the south side of the river, and each had a fine church building. These religions managed to survive in Iredell, although the many others that started up soon foundered through lack of both ministry and congregation. And even these remaining stalwart faiths were often dependent upon itinerant rather than local ministers.

Since these itinerant preachers couldn't always be there every Sunday, when they did come and hold services people were as happy for the excuse to gather as for the moral lesson they were certain to receive at the gathering. Often the preacher traveled twenty-five miles or more to hold a meeting, as did the settlers to hear him. It was a lonesome life and such meetings with friends made the loneliness a little more bearable. Aunt Clara spoke of it to me in this way, "Well, there were a lot of nice, good Christian people there, and of course it's like that all the way; the Lord makes some people hypocrites and some people good, and when I was a mighty little girl I came to find that out."

Her lovely mother was one of the good Christians, a Methodist, as it happens. "My mother was religious — not foolishly religious; she was a sensible woman, but she was a religious woman. And I got a start from her, and my father, he had to respect her religion too. But then, he was so honest anyway that he leaned backwards; he just always told his children that if they wanted to be anybody and have any respect for themselves, why the thing for them to do would be to treat their fellowmen like they'd like to be treated —" And in a special aside, she added, "You know that doesn't go very far in life these days, does it?"

Anyway, Mary McDonald saw to it that all of her brood went to church with her, and that they were obedient while there. She had beautiful brown eyes, and when any of the children was even slightly restive, she would just look at the offender, and he or she would promptly subside into silence and bodily quiet. She kept the current baby on her lap, the next youngest on a pallet at her side, and as soon as any was old enough to sit on the bench with her, that is where he sat — quietly. Clara and the others used to get very tired, as the "preacher would preach — oh, so long, and we'd get so tired. He'd do a lot of beating the air, you know, and hollering loud, and just going on and on — But we sat through it; we were trained to do that."

It is such a service that we visit in *Arbor Meeting,* for when the weather was particularly fine, the meeting was held in the open air. The Methodist church is in the background, and tied to trees and bushes in the middle ground are the horses and conveyances used by the members of the congregation to come to the meeting. A bit of whimsy on Aunt Clara's part has been to indicate, through these, every means of transportation then in use except for the train — surrey to wagon, hack to buggy to horseback, to the rowboat-ferry crossing the Bosque with its load of passengers, while others await their turn rather than trust to the stepping stones above the little falls.

It would seem that the meeting has been in progress for some time, for the expressions on the faces of the congregation are a bit glazed, and the two boys behind Mary McDonald have started to whisper and rough-house. She is still engrossed in the sermon, but we feel that her concentration will momentarily be broken, that she will turn to "look the boys into silence," as the preacher will apparently be beating the air for some time to come while the late arrivals join the meeting. Aunt Clara can tell who each person is in this painting, and his whole life history; and this individuality with which she has endowed her friends and neighbors of long ago makes them real for us today.

She also shows us *The Circuit Rider* himself, in another canvas, as he rides on horseback to keep his appointments around the countryside. This is Uncle Andrew Davis, who rode everywhere on horseback when he first started out, but, as he prospered, purchased a horse and buggy, and made his rounds in relative comfort. The usual distance traveled to hold a meeting was no longer than a day's ride, and one family or another who lived near the meeting-place would entertain the circuit-riding minister with food and rest and all the hospitality it was possible to offer. It was a mark of privilege to be the family to honor the minister in this manner, so all took turns in a most democratic way. When his schedule worked properly the traveling preacher would hold services in the various churches every other Sunday; but often the smaller and more distant communities waited longer than this for the preacher and the Word of God.

In the summer this need for spiritual stimulation was more than adequately fulfilled by the camp-meeting revivals. These were protracted prayer meetings that could last for several days to a week or more, going on day and night until the saved outnumbered the damned, and until exhaustion, both bodily and spiritual, finally halted the meeting — the weary, satiated participants going home replete.

Standing in the Need of Prayer shows one of the revival meetings that were held from time to time during the summer at Terrell Springs, right by Iredell. Since good water was readily and constantly available, this was an excellent campsite. The settlers came in from all around the countryside and set up their tents, built a fine arbor, and settled in for a big occasion of social interchange, spiced with wrestlings-with-the-devil and soul-saving on the grand scale. These prayer meetings were great occasions for the children, who looked forward to camping out, to the total change in routine and chores, and the fun of spending days and nights in close proximity to friends and cousins not often seen.

Here the moon has risen, the torches have been lit around the arbor, and Aunt Clara has achieved an extraordinary combination of this moonlight and torchlight in an atmosphere that immediately absorbs one into its excitement. She invites one also into the meeting by her uncanny placement of the aisle between the two benches in the foreground, and the back of the pigtailed girl as she starts in toward the prayer bench, with the viewer following. One is impelled to participate in the same manner as those who sit on the painted benches and breathe the heavy painted air; that perspire in the emotion-wrought searching and cleansing as the promise of salvation wreaks its spell. In the mat-black sky the stars even seem to twinkle, and one hears the music of the reed organ and the hallelujah singers. As in the *Arbor Meeting,* the congregation is made up of individuals, all well known. It makes no difference to Aunt Clara whether she paints

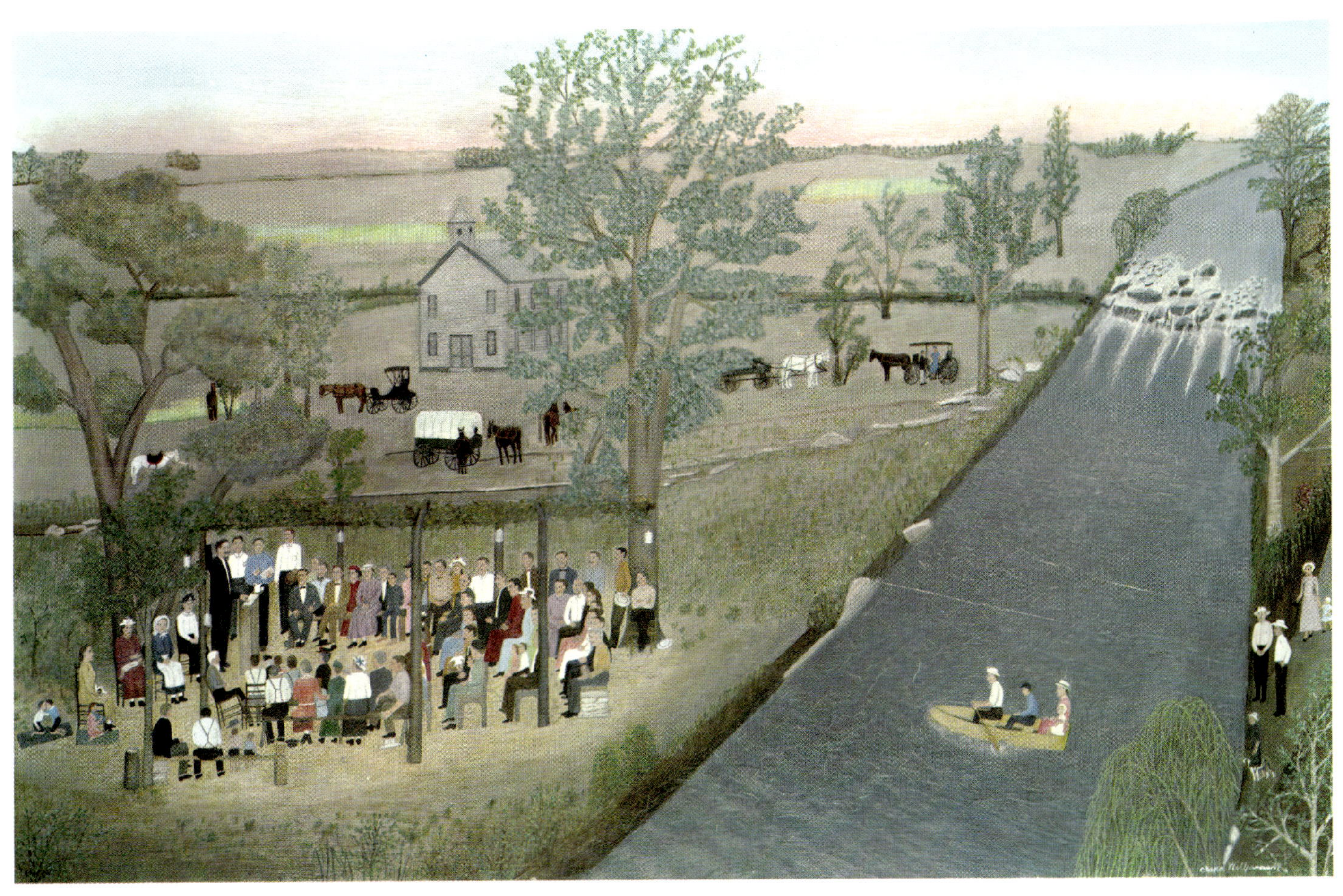

ARBOR MEETING
Oil on panel, 1957, 30 x 48 in.; courtesy Dr. and Mrs. Malcolm B. Bowers, Dallas

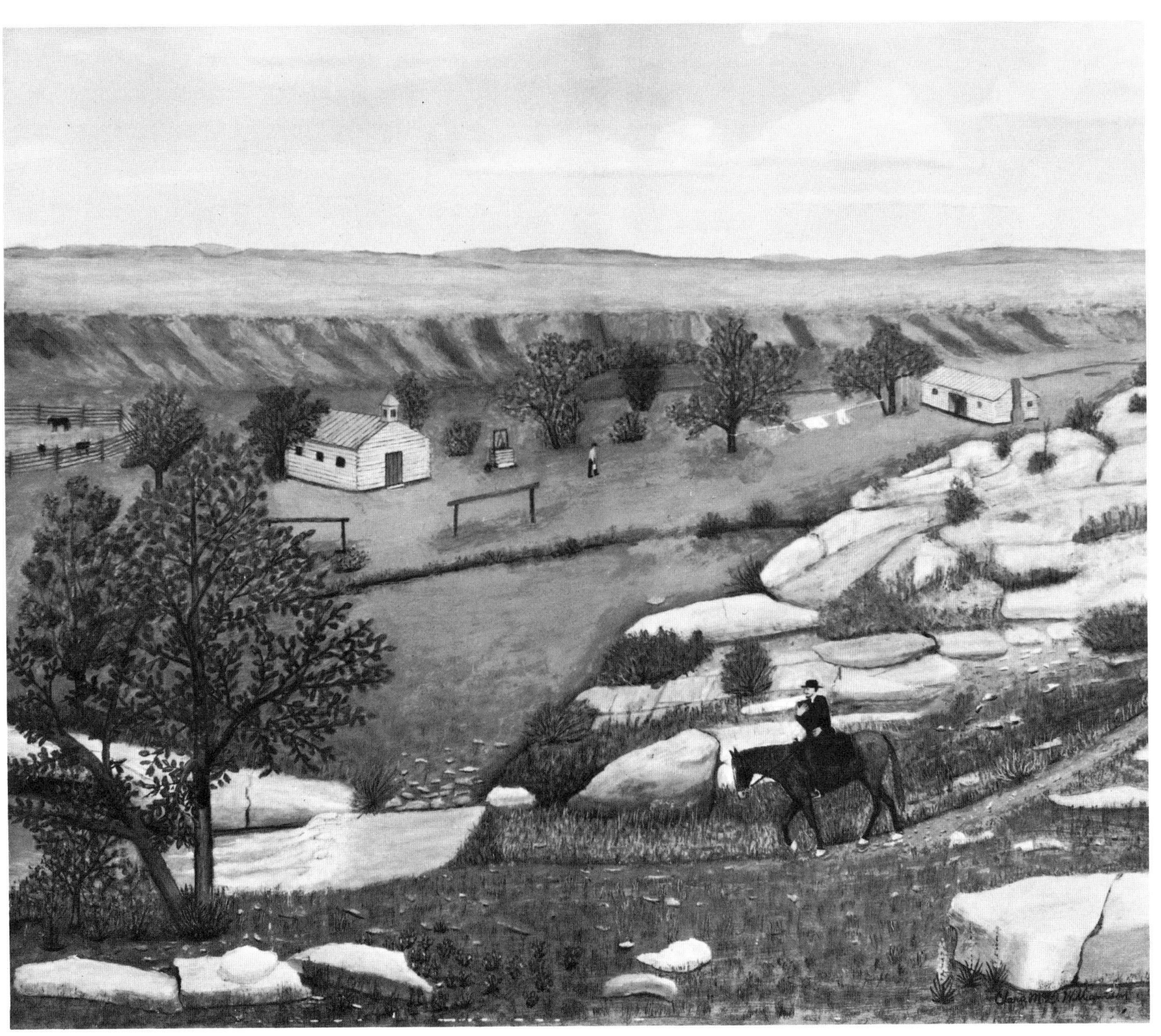

THE CIRCUIT RIDER
Oil on panel, 1955, 21 x 25 in.; courtesy Mr. and Mrs. H. Ben Decherd, Jr., Dallas

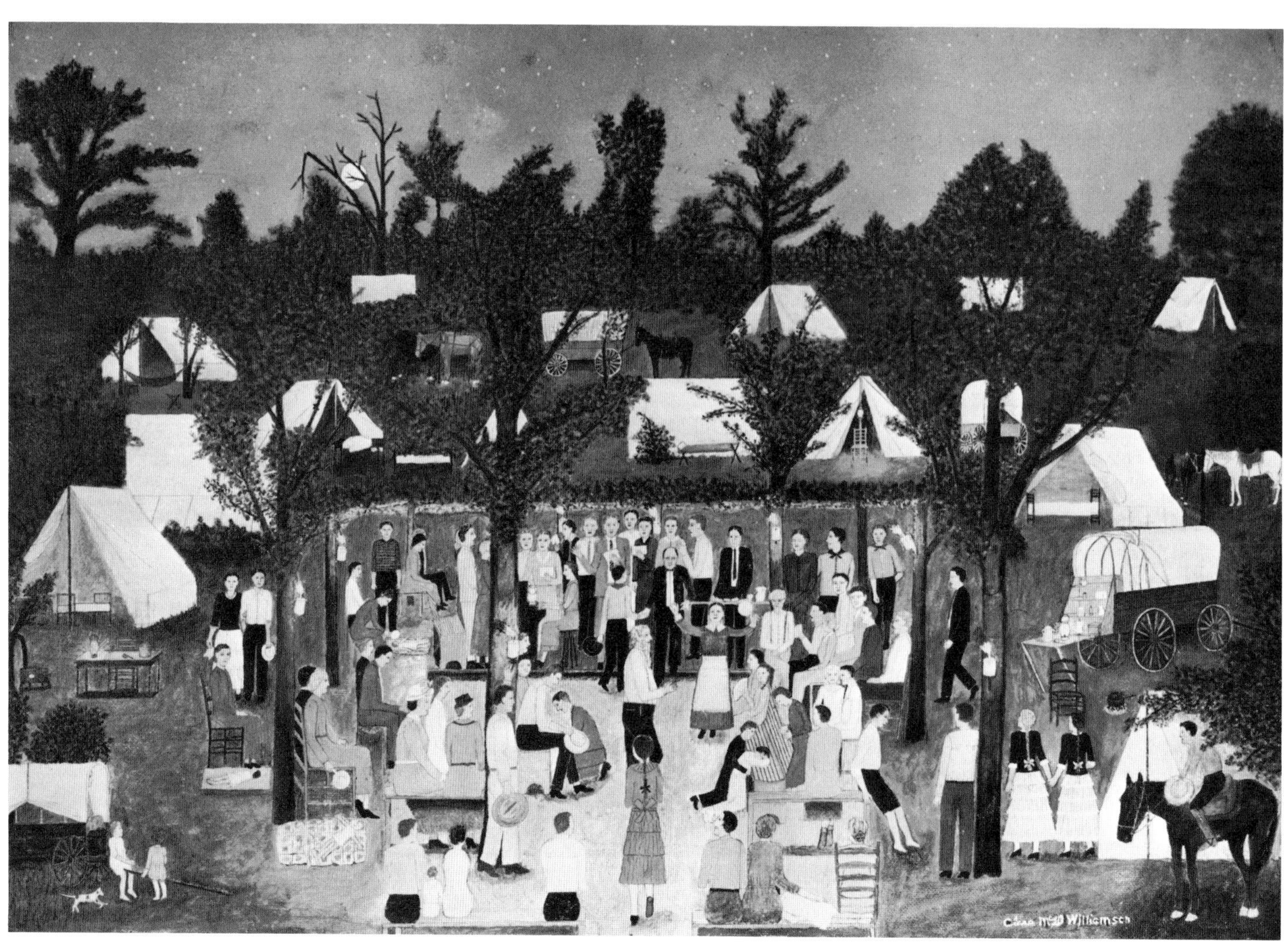

STANDING IN THE NEED OF PRAYER
Oil on panel, 1947, 28 x 40 in.; courtesy Mr. and Mrs. Dan C. Williams, Dallas

a crowd of people or one person; her memory is accurate for one or for all, and she paints as she remembers.

It is the child of the frontier that most concerns us when looking at Clara Williamson's paintings, for the greater part of her memory pictures are as seen through the eyes of such a child. It is this innocence and clarity of vision, the perfect remembrance of the pleasant, happy, or exciting things, that gives her work its freshness and untainted delight.

And this unblemished joyous vision is in itself miraculous, for the life she led as a child was far from pleasant. In our many talks together she often mentions that she does not look back on her childhood as a happy experience, though she says at the same time how devotedly she loved her mother and father, and of this we have much evidence. But parents in those days were just the reverse of what they are now. "You see, children in this day and time come first, and they are noticed and they're talked to and treated like intelligent human beings even when they're little — as fast as they grow up to it, you know. In that day and time, a child was supposed to stay out of sight and not talk around where the big people were; they weren't allowed to talk up about anything — you know, it was hard on children in my day — "

And it was particularly hard on little Clara, for besides being the eldest daughter ("Mother couldn't get any help in that place — so I was her help.") and being burdened from earliest childhood with heavy household responsibilities, she had a mother who was equally burdened, and a father who had little desire to spend time with his children. And her Grandfather Lasswell, who lived with them, that fine tall fellow, didn't like her. "He made life kind of hard on me, he wasn't good to me, and he didn't want me around him; so I stayed away from him all I could." She chuckles as she speaks of this now.

There is no resentment toward her people — only simple acceptance and a delicious humor as she evidently recalls with pleasure her

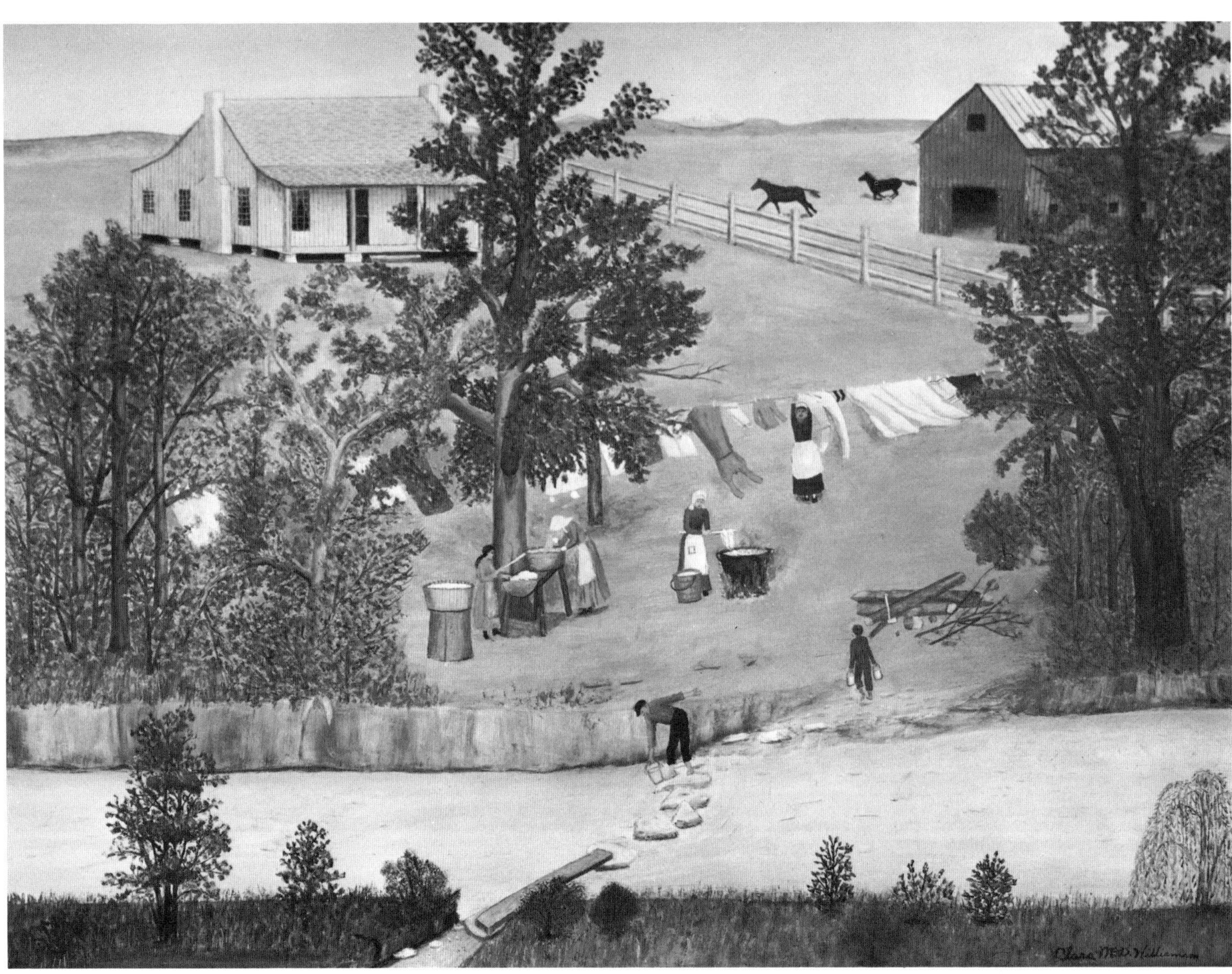

MONDAY
Oil on panel, 1955, 18 x 24 in.; courtesy Mr. and Mrs. John W. O'Boyle, Dallas

ways of "staying out of the way," even as she recalls the necessity for doing so. Her only resentment is that she was not able to receive the education she longed for so desperately, and that her opportunities of this sort were seriously curtailed by necessity and by the attitudes of that time. If she was needed at home, and she usually was, she just didn't get to go to school that day.

This habit of work was established long before she reached school age. Her painting *Monday* shows a whole family busily working together to get the family clothes clean, but, according to Aunt Clara, *she* was put to work at this chore when she was so small that she had to climb up on a chair to be tall enough to work at the split-log bench. Her mother would put the chair against the bench for her, and up she would climb to stay there the better part of a day washing the family's dirty clothes. These wooden washtubs banded in metal, and the split-log bench-tables, with the fence-post-size legs spraddling out on either side, were part of her father's stock in trade, and she knew them well. As Clara grew older she participated in the other washday jobs shown in the painting: carrying the water, boiling the clothes, standing to the wash bench, doing the rinsing, then hanging the clothes on the line.

In further revelation of the work the children were required to do is Aunt Clara's idyllic painting of the evening chores, *Chore Time.* Here all is pastoral pleasure: the animals and the fields are fertile, the cow is being milked, the chickens and other fowl are being fed, and the water is being drawn from the well as the father rides home to this industrious and peaceful scene. It is the lull at evening, no wind stirs, and nothing mars the illusion of total harmony.

But what this particular child yearned to do was to go to school and to be permitted to attend regularly. Actually, schooling for most of the children was a matter of catch-as-catch-can, for the needs of the family overbore the need for learning. A church building served during the week as a schoolhouse, with all the grades in one room under the tutelage of one benighted teacher, who came up from Waco. ABC's to algebra and geometry were taught concurrently, and the blackboards might well encompass all at the same time, with a bit of verb parsing thrown in. A "mixed school" is what she calls it.

Aunt Clara recalls with the usual vivid detail her first marvelous day at school. She was torn between pleasurable excitement and fright, and when the whole school stood while they recited the multiplication table in turn, she (with no preparation) recited the whole table when it came to her turn "without hardly even thinking about it at all." She feels that no one took her very seriously at school and hardly noticed that she was there, but I feel certain the dedicated man who taught these children must have been very impressed by this exceptional child with her uncannily retentive memory and her ability to stay abreast of her group and even ahead of them, although she was absent so frequently. She speaks of this ability, "Well, I just absorbed it, I honestly just inherited it; I didn't learn it, you know. I didn't go to school much.

"I'll tell you how I went to school. I'd get to go maybe two days in a week, and then I'd have to miss three days of school. Then, if Mama needed me, if any of the little brothers or sisters got sick, well, I'd stay at home three or four days a week. Sometimes I only went one day. I went to school when I got a chance to. I had to work and wash and iron and take care of my little brothers and sisters, and then I'd go back. I know they used to laugh about it, and say — well, I could stay out so long, but when I got back I knew as much as the rest of the class — I don't think I did, but anyway, I kept up with them. It wasn't like it is now — to get a tutor or go to summer school — I just had to catch up and learn it."

The course of study and reading pursued was laid out in the McGuffey *Readers,* of which Aunt Clara said — "I went clear up the line on that reader, and you know the world would be better off if they still started children out to read in it — All through those readers they had such a wonderful and beautifully expressed moral lesson that went clear through the *Fifth Reader,* I think. They would always give a good, wholesome, pleasing moral lesson out of it, and when I was a child I just ate them up."

And she "ate up" every book she could get into her eager hands, including the yellow-backed novels, smuggled into the house by her bookworm of an older brother. The only retreat at home where she could read undiscovered was under her bed. Whenever she had completed a particular task she would slip off from her mother and crawl back under the bed, where, as she admits, she could hardly see, and read whatever book she had managed to borrow, or that was handed on from her brother. She mentions in particular *The Lady of the Lake* and *The Last of the Mohicans,* along with the more lurid yellowbacks. Her brother Allen, having hung around the train depot from the time it was built, and having learned telegraphy from the operator there, went to work for the railroad at the age of fourteen as a telegrapher. So his comparative affluence and love of reading brought many books into the house to be passed on to little Clara.

She speaks of the way she managed time to read. "You know, my mother, she'd keep me so busy, and I'd take that book, and when I'd get something done that she told me to do — well, I'd go and do it, and then I'd scoot right out and I'd disappear and I'd crawl down under that bed with that book and read. And then she'd commence a-calling, 'Clara, Clara, where are you?' and I'd have to, quick, put my book down so I could find my place again and crawl out from under that bed and go arunning to her. And for the longest time she didn't know where I'd hide to read, and she'd say, 'What in the world are you doing? Stay in here and do this — I need you!' and so I'd do that, and first thing you know, back I'd go to my book."

Besides the lure of the world of books, *The Gordon Schoolhouse* gives us an excellent idea of some of the other enticements to attend school. For here she has shared with us the joy of the recess periods, the social time for children who had very little of it. Although Clara did not attend the Gordon School, which was a good distance north of Iredell and her home, her brothers did from time to time, and in this painting of it she has recorded many of the games and recess pastimes they all enjoyed the most.

We see the perennial running or scuffling boys, the game of stickball well in progress; a gentle interlude with the swing, and a cooling drink of water being drawn from the well; we see the smaller children with their supervised "Ring Around the Rosey." But the game that little Clara enjoyed the most and excelled in was a game called "Wolf over the river," which is being played in the middle ground of the painting, just below and to the right of the schoolhouse. Clara was exceptionally fleet-footed, and in this game of capture and chase

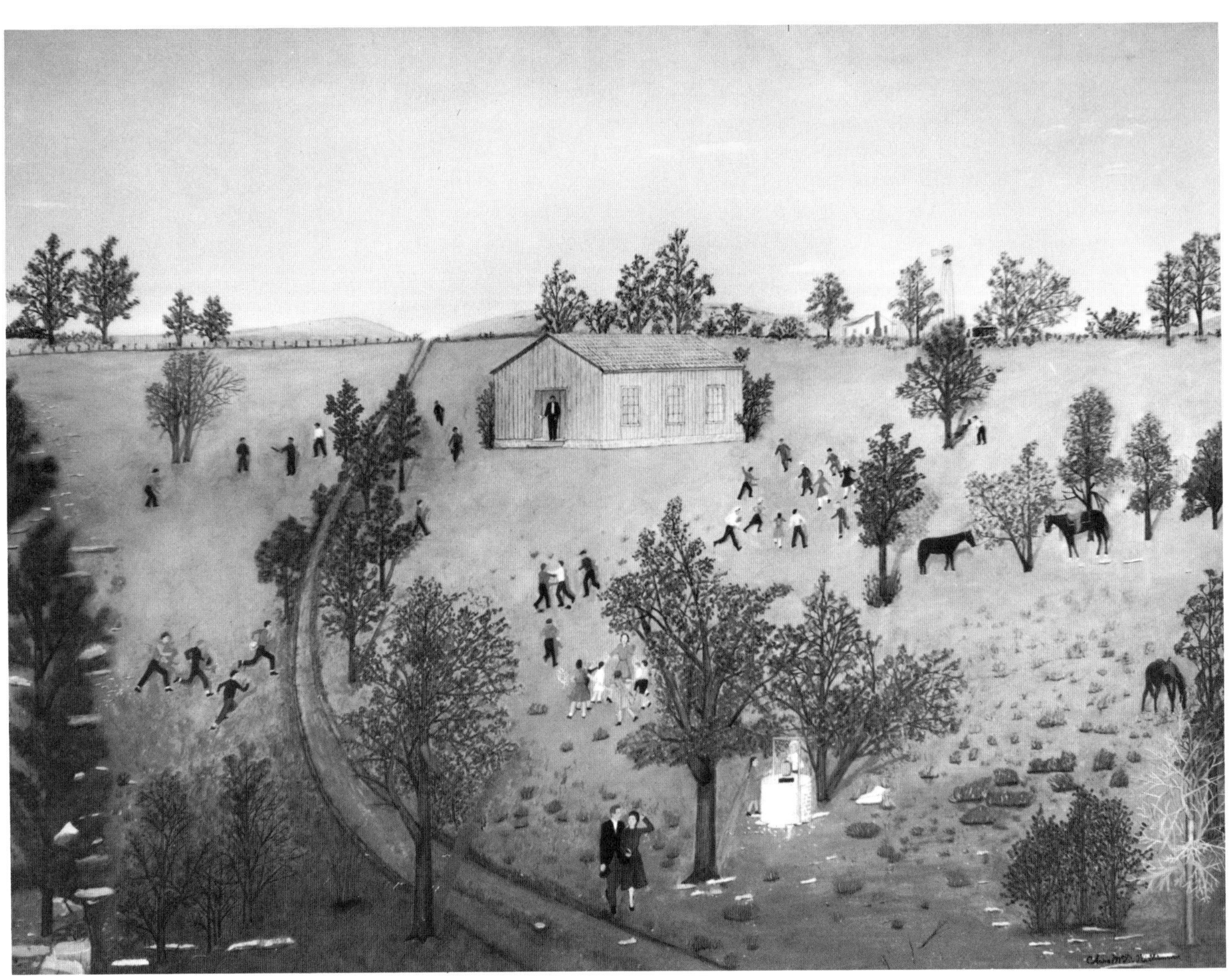

THE GORDON SCHOOLHOUSE
Oil on panel, 1960-1961, 30 x 40 in.; courtesy Valley House Gallery, Dallas

she too often beat the boys. They didn't enjoy finding out over and over that she could outrun them — could dodge the wolf and get over the river no matter how many ran after her.

She and the other children also greatly enjoyed play-dancing, and "set to" with much energy and rhythm to the music of their own singing. One of the favorite songs to which they danced was "See Sally Goodin," in which one of the lines ran, "Thought to my soul I'd kill myself arunning." So it is easy to visualize the energetic nature of the dance and its popularity with Clara.

The delights of "after school" and the route home often rivalled those of the recess. One of these, the more attractive for being forbidden, was a stop at the marvelous *Blacksmith Shop* before crossing the river on the way home. This was owned by Mr. Bateman, who was a kindly man. He was also very strong, as is the tradition and necessity of smithing. He forbade the children to come around the shop only for fear that they would pick up nails in their bare feet.

From the painting one can see how well the children heeded this warning. It was such a fascinating place that they couldn't resist coming; they were always running around the side of the shop and peeping around the corner, listening and watching as long as they could before the inevitable discovery; hoping their presence would go unnoticed and that just this once Mr. Bateman wouldn't order them off. It was a treat for the children to see the handsome horses, to watch the shoeing ritual, to watch the exciting alternate flaring and waning of the fire in the forge, and, mainly, to hear the conversations among the men and the stories that were told over and over until they became an integral part of the history of the town.

One such story was the quite fabulous tale of Mr. Loader and how he won the hand of a lady-in-waiting to Queen Victoria, and how they came and settled in Iredell. Clara must have heard this story from the time she was very tiny, as Mr. Loader became the first postmaster of Iredell, and was the man who registered the name of the town with the federal government in Washington. The story as I have heard it from Aunt Clara many, many times, goes very much like this:

A second-cousin of Queen Victoria, who served as one of her ladies-in-waiting, fell in love with a commoner, a shipbuilder in England, by the name of John Loader. One of the young woman's tasks was to see that Queen Victoria's bed was made without a wrinkle; that

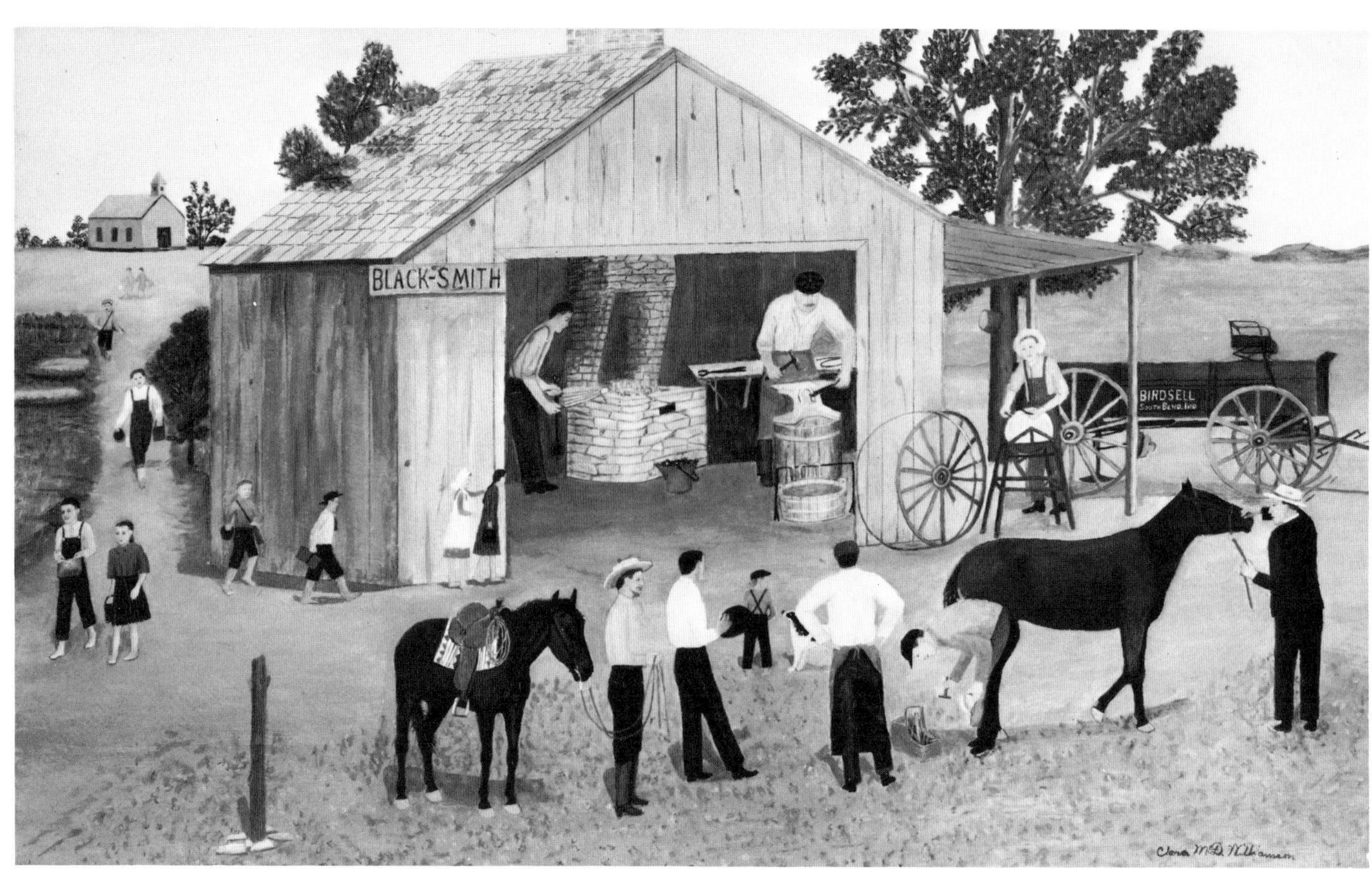

THE BLACKSMITH SHOP
Oil on panel, 1955, 18 x 30 in.; courtesy Dr. and Mrs. P. M. Williamson, Dayton, Ohio

the sheets were "oh, so tight and smooth — so smooth —" Naturally, no consent could be given to such a match between the high and the low; so the lovers decided to elope. The lady-in-waiting (she is never referred to in any other manner) had some close friends who were about to take passage for America, and she prevailed upon them to take her and her young man with them. Since the friends had a generous sympathy for this couple, they somehow managed to pack John Loader into a goods box ("You know the colonies had to buy a lot of things from England they couldn't get here; so lots of goods boxes were coming over all the time"), and packed in this manner, he made the crossing of the Atlantic on the same ship as his lady love.

It is at this point that the story becomes somewhat confusing, as one is left in doubt as to whether Mr. Loader came out of the goods box on his arrival in America, or whether the goods box was shipped intact on to Iredell. Aunt Clara is rather indefinite about this, no matter how many times she tells the story, and one version goes that "when they got there, they just un-nailed the goods box, and he popped out, and they got married." This is the version that most appeals to me. The young couple did somehow manage to go overland to Iredell, and the presence of this English couple gave the town a particular "class."

A further note to be added is that the Loaders never communicated with the royal relatives in England, and when some word finally came to them it was the sad news that the young lady's mother had died of a broken heart. Surely no more romantic tale could charm the thoughts of a plain, impressionable frontier child. Little Clara knew Mrs. Loader well, and found her a graceful little woman. She was present on one occasion when the lady got up to show her guests how they had danced when she had attended balls at the Royal Court. She "tripped around so fantastically, and was oh, so quiet — she was so light on her feet you could hear a pin drop — nobody stomped when *they* danced —" It was like having a princess in one's own home town!

Having dawdled along the way home from school as long as she dared, Clara would run up the hill and in the front door to find *The Family Room,* much as she has pictured it for us. Her mother and some friends are working cotton into thread and cloth; the evening meal is cooking over the fire and on the hearth; the cat sleeps happily in the warmth. The table is partially set; Clara will complete the setting now that she is home from school, and busy herself with the

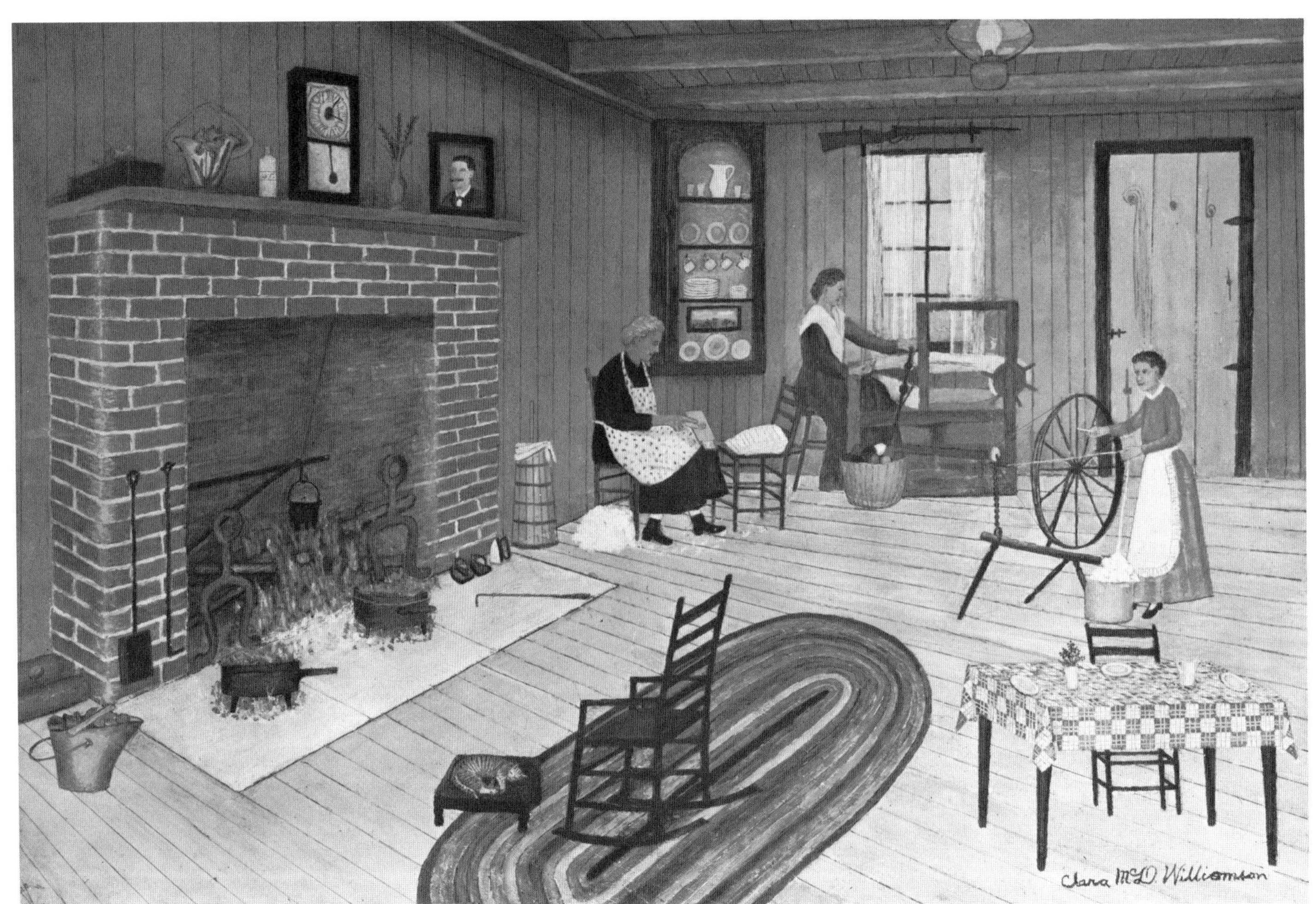

THE FAMILY ROOM
Oil on panel, 1955, 15 x 22½ in.; courtesy Dr. and Mrs. P. M. Williamson, Dayton, Ohio

other early-evening chores daily required of her. It has always been of interest to me to find the family clock which one sees on the mantel in the painting, still ticking accurately and chiming the hours from the mantel of Aunt Clara's present home, a constant reminder of the house on the hill and the main living room in which most of the family activities took place.

On fine spring and summer evenings, after the supper dishes were washed, and the other evening chores completed, came the best time of each day, when the whole family could gather outside in front of the house, and relax and visit together. This was the peaceful and quiet time, when it was daylight up to Clara's bedtime, and beyond it, and when the family enjoyed together the coming of twilight. In *A Day's Work Is Done* we meet the family that gathered so often at the McDonald Place, as the house on the hill is still called by the Iredell community.

Clara and her sister Addie (once again dressed in pink because she was "such a pretty thing") are playing Stiff-Starch in the foreground, clasping hands and whirling around and round to see who could get "drunk" the quickest. In a moment we know that one of them will fall to the ground, rolling and giggling, until she can stand up without "tilting" and start around again. Passing the oblivious girls is their dressed-up older brother, Allen, who is leaving for a date with a young lady. Aunt Clara remembers that he was "waiting on Liz Mingus around that time, so he was probably going over to her place." Sister Annabel is chasing her cousin, who has pulled off her hair ribbon and is teasing her with it.

The focus of attention is the two babies, rolling and grabbing, who have just fallen from the lower step in their play. The dark one is baby brother Tommy, and the fair one is a cousin, Lee Lasswell. His mother, Aunt Adaline, is rushing down the steps to help the babies, while Lee's father, the man in the suit, also reaches for them. Uncle Joe (in the cowboy hat to the right of the babies) is also getting out of his seat to see if he can be of any assistance in separating the small wrestlers. (Aunt Clara always refers to her Uncle Joe, whom the children adored, as either "my bachelor uncle" or "my wicked cowboy uncle — he never married, you know — only one of the family never married.") Clara's mother is coming out of the house to see what all the noise is about; her father in his shirtsleeves and vest, sits on the porch undisturbed by the ruckus, and Grandfather Lass-

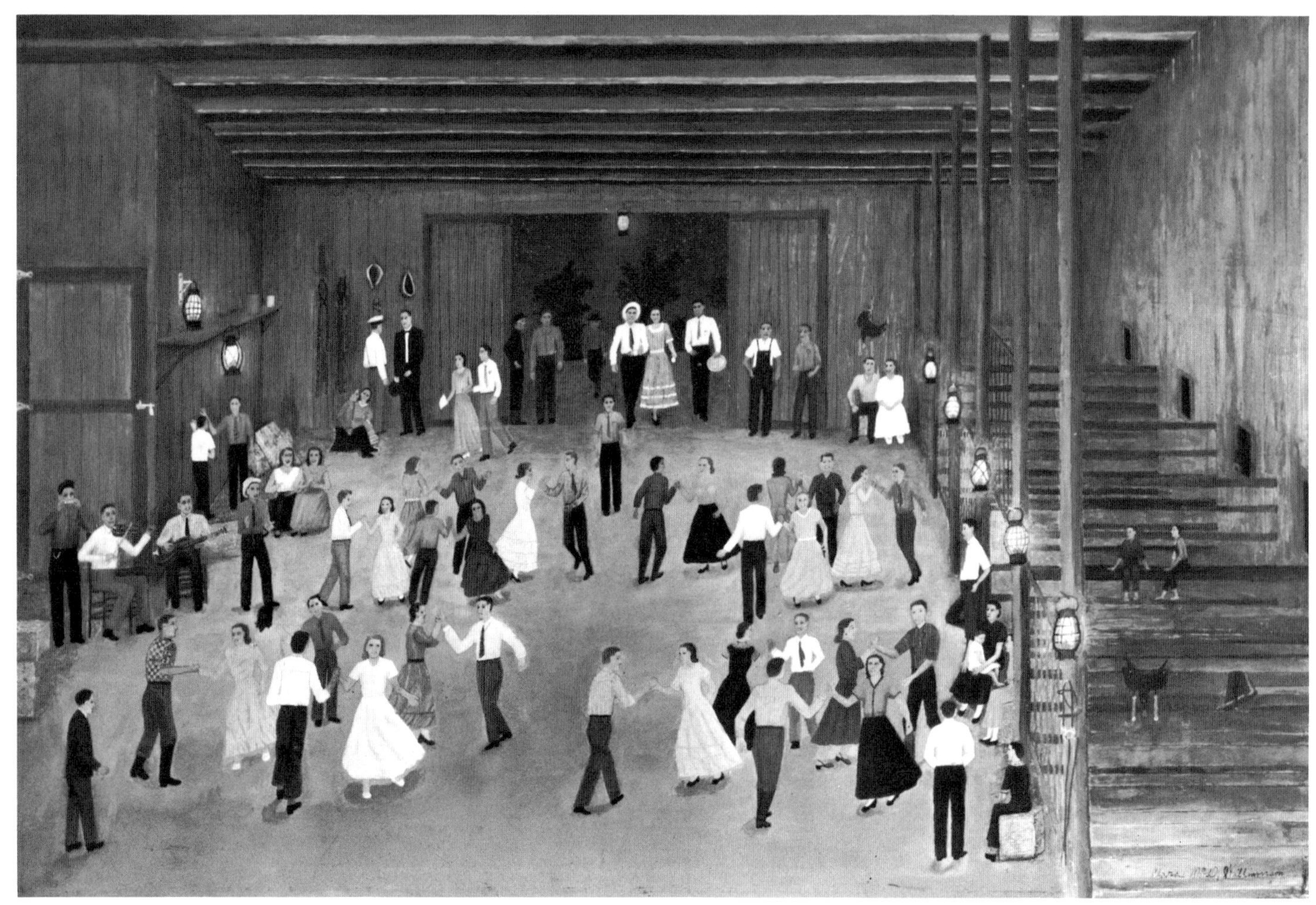

TEXAS BARN DANCE
Oil on panel, 1951, 24 x 36 in.; courtesy Dr. and Mrs. Malcolm B. Bowers, Dallas

well, equally unruffled, is the great tall man with the white beard and the cane. Next to him, on the ground, stands a disinterested younger brother, James Alexander, who seems undecided as to whether it would be more fun to get involved with teasing Annabel about her missing hair ribbon, or to interfere in the game of Stiff-Starch. And so we meet Clara's family.

A Day's Work Is Done is a prime example of Aunt Clara's gift of differentiation between the animate and the inanimate in her work. The house, the red picket fence, the chairs, are stolidly and marvelously inanimate — they are as unalive as her family is alive for us in this painting. The vitality and the animation of the living is always in true contrast and relation to the inanimate. Whether she paints a horse or a cow, a cat or chicken, a child or other person, these creatures all live and move and breathe and react in opposition, let us say, to a house, a building, the ground or a mountain. There is an implicit sense of air that is breathed in all of her paintings; air that can in a moment turn into a breeze to stir the branches of the trees, turn the windmill, riffle the hair of the people moving through her canvases. Not only the animation of what is immediately occurring is communicated, but anticipation of what will happen next. And she is masterly in her manifestation of these concepts.

Among the purely social gatherings, unmarked by religious overtones, the barn dance was an event to be anticipated for weeks with pleasurable excitement and preparation. It was a family affair, including the smallest baby and the oldest grandparent — for those who were too young or too old to enjoy the admittedly athletic dancing found almost equal enjoyment in watching the show and in gossiping about the participants.

Aunt Clara's *Texas Barn Dance* re-creates for us these country revels and permits one to become an excited participant in them. As she indicates, the barns of her day were very well built, for horses and milk cows were important to the settlers, and they often made their barns before they built decent homes for their families. When such a barn was cleaned up a bit, with the horses and cattle turned out for the night, it made a fine dance hall. The friends and neighbors for some distance around were invited, and as the families arrived (after greetings all around) the smallest children would be bedded down on fresh hay in the stalls, some being already asleep from the long drive in to the dance. Others, older and awake and eager, would dance on the edges of the squares a bit themselves before being relegated to the stalls, where (if they remained wakeful, and if the warning eyes of parents could be avoided) they could climb to perch on the rails and watch well into the night.

The band might be composed of a violin, a guitar, and a harmonica, as is the band in the painting, or a French harp might take the place of, or augment, the harmonica. The caller called for the whole room; so all the dancers in all the squares would be doing the same figure in the dance at the same time. This unity of pattern creates a most stimulating and vigorous rhythm in the painting.

Besides providing a welcome community evening for whole families who lived in isolated, lonely units much of the time, the barn dance also supplied a fallow ground for courtships and pairings-off. Since opportunity for this activity was sparse in the pioneer towns — and even then often under the watchful patronage of the church — the privacy and freedom proffered by the atmosphere of the barn dance was exceptionally welcome. And a cooling walk under the stars with one's partner or another eligible young person was frequently the deciding factor in whether a proposal of marriage would be offered, and whether it would be accepted or rejected. The couple coming through the doors open to the stars at the back of the painting look as if some such decision has just been reached.

Other exciting asides were likely to occur. One such story concerns the sagacity of the sheriff of northern Bosque County at the time that Clara was a girl; a very nice man named Bill Boyd, who knew his business well, and who was a "great detective."

It seems that three teen-aged boys one night got together. Feeling like some devilment and being short of cash, they decided to rob old Brother Roberts ("a good old frontier Baptist preacher"). In the middle of the burglary Aunt Fanny Roberts, the preacher's wife, was awakened by the noise and started screaming, frightening the boys

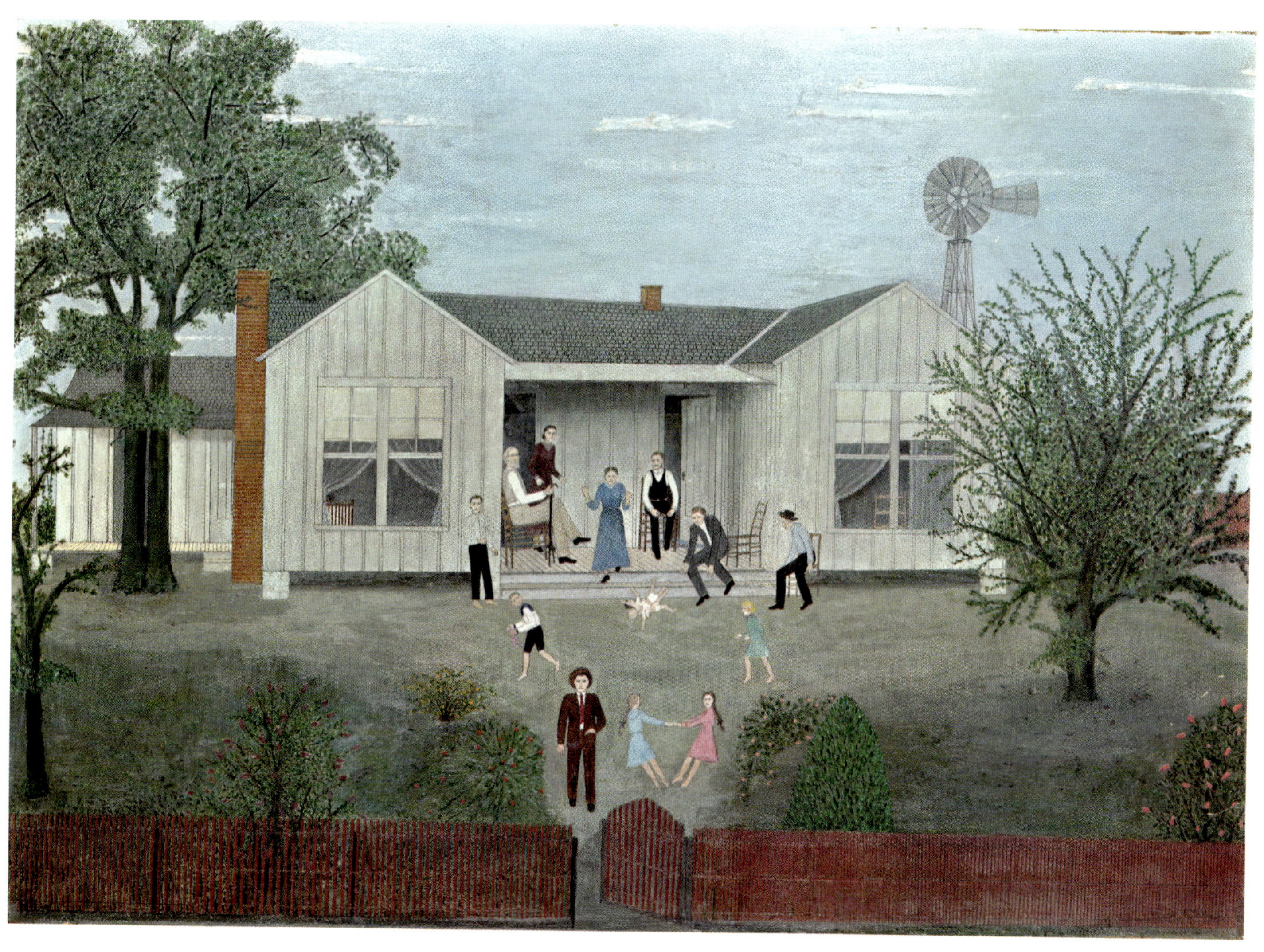

A DAY'S WORK IS DONE
Oil on panel, 1946, 28 x 39¾ in.; courtesy Amon Carter Museum, Fort Worth

away. Snatching up what they had already collected, they ran so fast and it was so dark that no one could identify the boys, and for some long time, no one knew who did it. But the wise Sheriff Boyd had no intention of permitting this mystery to go unsolved, and he started going to all the dances around and about, knowing that the boys were certain to show up at one or another of these.

One night, having a certain intuitive feeling during such a barn dance, the sheriff climbed a tree under which he knew it was customary for young men to gather after each dance, to cool off. Again it was very dark, but this time the sheriff couldn't be seen. "And those boys came up under that tree and talked it all out, the whole robbery, and the sheriff heard it all, and jumped down out of the tree and arrested them." There was no jail in Iredell, so he had to take them to the jailhouse at the county seat, Meridian, around twelve miles away. They were duly tried, found guilty, and sent off for a while.

But so great was the remorse of one of the boys, a Bud Mitchell, that when he was ready to get married, he took his bride-to-be in a buggy right to old Brother Robert's house, "and Bud called him out and he married them settin' there in the buggy. He made a nice man when he was grown up."

Among the most historically interesting of her memory paintings are those in the series concerning the native longhorn cattle, the cattle drives, and the cowboys. One of Iredell's claims to existence, and certainly one of its reasons for growing into such a prosperous little community, was its situation as a stopover on the Chisholm Trail, and as a child Clara was intimately concerned with the Texas longhorn, of which she readily admits to being just a bit afraid. Her cousins ran cattle, and her bachelor Uncle Joe was a cowboy, and a fair portion of the town's economy was based on the many cattle drives that in season came one after the other for a night's stop in Iredell.

Two of her important pictures deal with these forced migrations of cattle as they ford the Bosque in and out of Iredell: *Git 'Long Little Dogies* and *The Old Chisholm Trail.* In the former we watch with

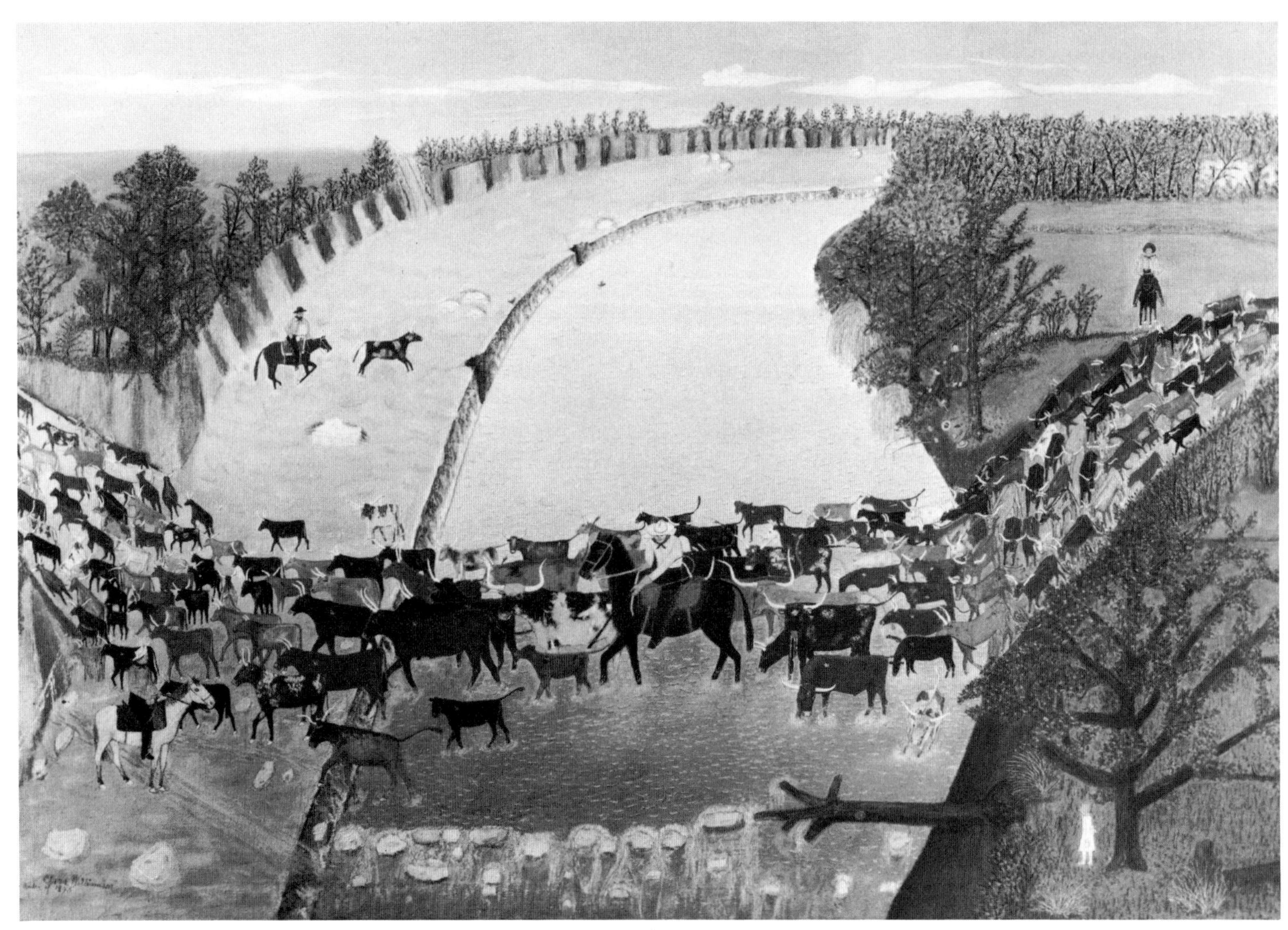

GET ALONG LITTLE DOGIES (GIT 'LONG LITTLE DOGIES)
Oil on canvas, 1945, 26¾ x 39¾ in.; courtesy Dallas Museum of Fine Arts, Dallas

Clara as she stands under a sheltering tree at a safe distance from the large beasts with their huge horns. The cowboys guide them in a masterly manner as they cross in the still water above the falls. A poke or prod is enough to keep them moving steadily. A steer founders, but will soon regain his footing; a cowboy readies his rope as he chases a vagrant; two small boys interrupt their fishing to watch the excitement from a precarious perch on the branch of a tree.

The Old Chisholm Trail might portray the same drive, as seen head-on, instead of from the side. Instead of a close-up from the riverbank, we see the long, stretching herd, just clear of the mountains, as they are guided into the valley of the Bosque and of Iredell. The lead cattle seem ready to stop and graze, uninclined to any mischief. In speaking of these paintings of cattle and cowboys Aunt Clara once said, "I wish I'd made them right while I was at it. When I look at some of my old pictures — well, I can find mistake after mistake in the one the Dallas Museum has *(Git 'Long Little Dogies). The Old Chisholm Trail* is better. I really got the Texas longhorns right in that one."

There are many others to supplement the two we have reproduced, each with its own captured moment of cow and cowboy: *Bulldogging, Mother Love on the Range, Early Texas Cowboy, Monarch of the Range, Riding and Roping on the Range* ("Uncle Joe is going to miss that yearling with the rope, you know"), and many others. It is a subject as fascinating to her as it becomes to us through her paintings.

The Bosque River, so easily forded by the cattle and horses, and by the children who happily hopped from stone to stone across it on the way to school or church, could not always be counted on as a pleasant and manageable mainstream in the life of Iredell. As with most Texas rivers, the Bosque, when swollen with suddenly heavy rains, periodically became a perilous neighbor, swift, ugly, and muddily dangerous. But in all the ninety years that Aunt Clara has known it,

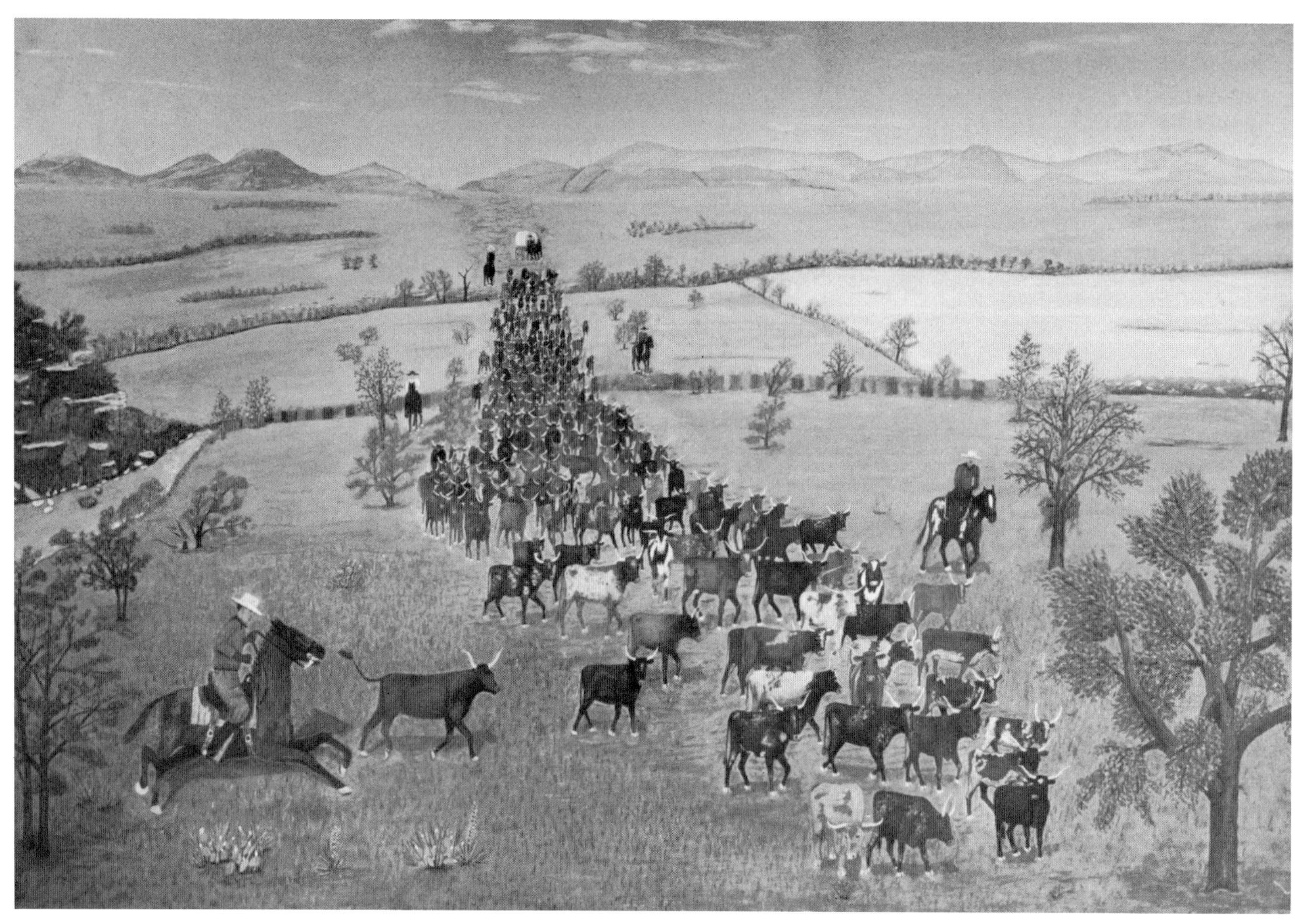

OLD CHISHOLM TRAIL
Oil on panel, 1952, 24 x 36½ in.; courtesy Wichita Art Museum, Roland P. Murdock Collection, Wichita, Kansas

the Bosque perpetrated only one real treachery — known to all as THE FLOOD.

The great tragedy occurred one spring morning when Clara was around ten. The waters of the Bosque, fed by heavy rains upriver, and the equally burgeoning waters of the Duffau, suddenly rose to spread across the whole valley, claiming everything in its path, sparing nothing. From her safety in the house on the hill Clara woke to the roar of the waters and the cries of her neighbors as they ran to the hill for safety. There was time to save nothing but life, and the miracle was that no one drowned. Nearly everyone from the town rushed from the danger to gather on her hill, and from this place of refuge and vantage point Clara watched the devastation with them.

Cry followed cry as one family after another saw everything they owned being washed away; in particular she remembers seeing her uncle's home simply burst in two, and her aunt fainting at this sight and being caught by a neighbor standing near. "The black waters rolled by clear over the whole valley and touched the foot of the hill where my home was. Uncle Joe was one of the last to leave the depot platform, and as he swam his horse to the base of the hill, and the horse scrambled out to shake the water from his coat, Uncle Joe yelled out, 'That damned store's bursting all apart!' — He was pretty wicked, used bad language, you know."

They all watched a man across on the southern bank of the river, chaining oxen to his home and to the immense sycamore trees that grew beside the river, with the obvious idea of using them all to hold his house from washing away. Aunt Clara's comment on this as she told me of it was, "Wasn't that foolish, now? The house burst open with all the rest, and the trees went, too." It was twenty-four hours before the water receded enough for the pitiful rescuing of keepsakes and the inevitable cleaning up.

The treachery was total: the town of Iredell ("prettiest town you ever saw before The Flood") was literally washed away. This town that we have become acquainted with through so many of Aunt Clara's paintings of it exists no longer. After The Flood another Iredell was built on the higher south side of the river, where it remains today, its existence never to be endangered to any extent by high water.

The graphic descriptions of The Flood that Aunt Clara has often given me formed such vivid mental pictures that I asked her why she had never painted it or anything relating to it. Her revealing answer was, "Yes, I guess it's a picture I *should* paint — if it wasn't destruction, I'd tackle it some day." And a few minutes later, "Some things you don't want to put down on canvas — they're too hectic."

And instead of painting The Flood on the Bosque she has painted perhaps the loveliest of her many delightful "imaginings." It is called *The Dream,* and pictorializes a dream she actually had, in which she floated above the river, following it downstream for quite a distance. She saw beneath her the cool clarity of the water, moving along with her, far, far, below, and the huge sycamore trees, with their mammoth foliage, most of which were later washed away by The Flood. She says that she forgot her body, and that the sensation which she magically communicates as we drift with her over the river was exactly the same as that which she felt some fifty-odd years later when she flew for the first time on a plane.

With all the great respect and knowledge I have concerning Clara Williamson's instinctive adroitness with brush and paint and canvas, I still find the particular magic with which she has imbued this painting almost incredible. For somehow she wraps one in her dream; the sensitive viewer is with deft surety transported along with the dreaming child, moving with the flow of the water beneath, the floating sensation becoming more pronounced the longer one participates in the painting. I can only marvel that she apparently finds it so simple to make such a translation come about.

In summer, many of the children's pastimes continued to center around the Bosque. When the youngsters were not engaged in the omnipresent chores and work, the enticements proffered by streams and pools of water in the hot Texas summers were ready magnets. The obvious pleasures of wading, swimming, and fishing were augmented by the lure of exploration along the banks with the many discoveries there to be made; the picnics on the large, flat rocks that ledged into the water far enough so that one could cool one's feet in the water while eating, and the cottonwoods that edged the streams, lending themselves to aerial exploits as well as to derring-do on swinging grapevines, and simple shade for the less brave and athletic.

Clara, being more curious than most, was an explorer of the riverbanks whenever she could slip away from home and the care of the smaller brothers and sisters. It was on one such hot day that she came across a group of boys swimming at the Ira Keeler Hole in the Bosque. (It was so deep that any deep hole became known in those parts as a "Keeler hole," and when occasionally a boy from the community accidentally drowned, it was said that he "fell in a Keeler hole.") Clara had just hidden herself behind a tree for some spying, when the classic drama of young ladies arriving at a river bank to be shocked by young men swimming in the altogether, revealed itself to her recording eye and mind.

This is the story of *The Girls Went Fishing,* and rarely, if ever, has the story been so well and graphically told. The total surprise of the girls who had come to the river for some quiet fishing and gossip, their hands raised in shocked gesture as the can of worms and fishing poles fall unheeded to the ground (or rather, in the painting, pause in mid-air to create the tension of arrested movement) is countered excitingly by the equal surprise of the boy who has snatched up his shirt as he runs wildly in the opposite direction, followed by the splashing, swimming boys in the water. The racing lad is held from flying off the canvas only by the figure of the modest boy in the center, who has simply stepped from the water to the shelter of the protective bushes along the bank.

Aunt Clara admits readily that she was really spying on the boys, but that her sister and friends came upon them by accident, being almost on top of the boys before realizing that they were there at all. When I teased Mrs. Williamson about being such a bold young lady, she gave her delicious chuckle and said, "I saw a lot, but I kept my mouth shut."

And the action and drama and humor that she has communicated so well in this painting of an event in which she participated is interestingly missing in a much later painting called *At the Old Swimming Hole,* which is an idyllic imagining of what such a place might be like. In the latter painting the figures of the young men and boys are

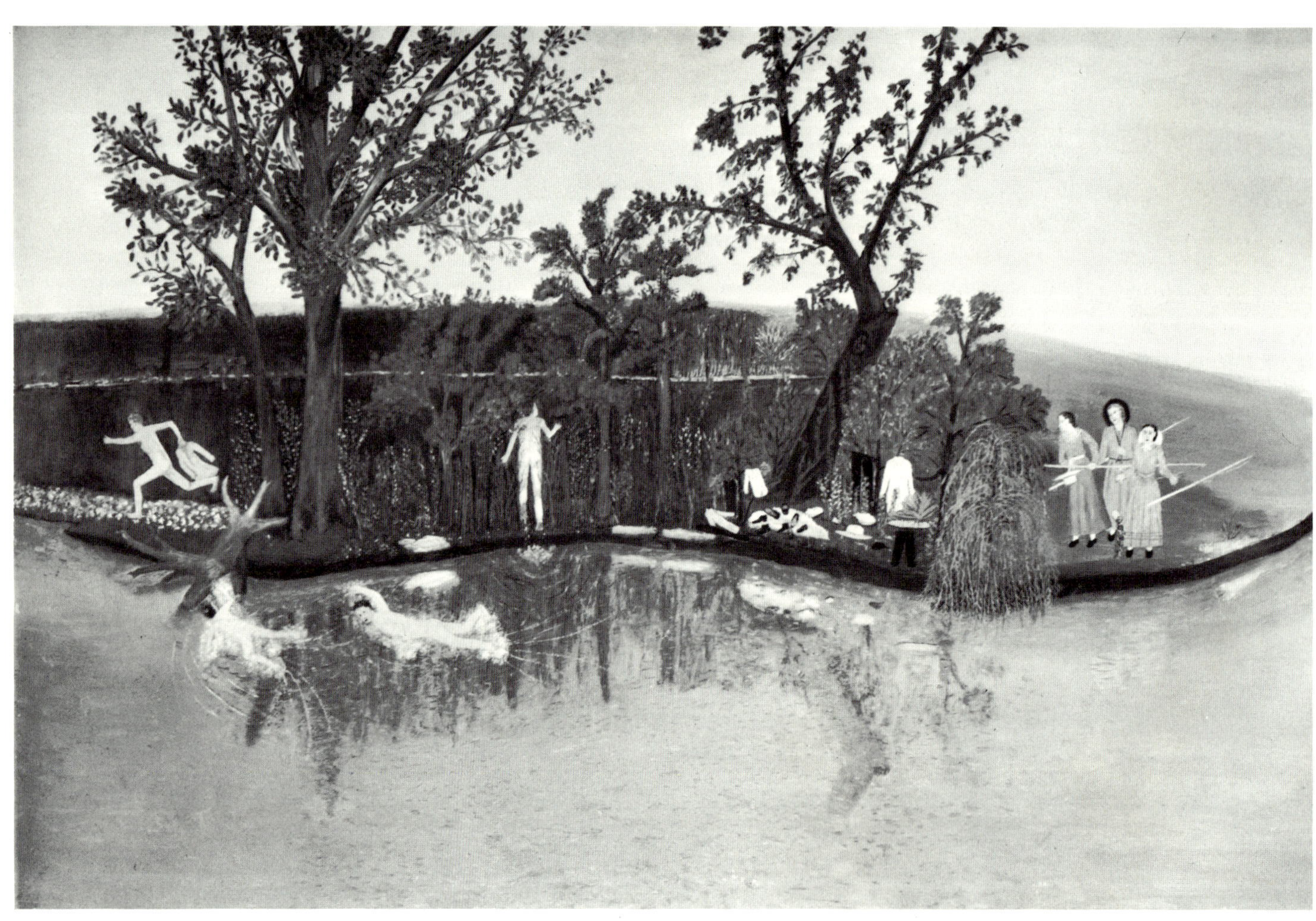

THE GIRLS WENT FISHING
Oil on canvas, 1945-1946, 24 x 36½ in.; courtesy John R. McLean, West Palm Beach, Florida

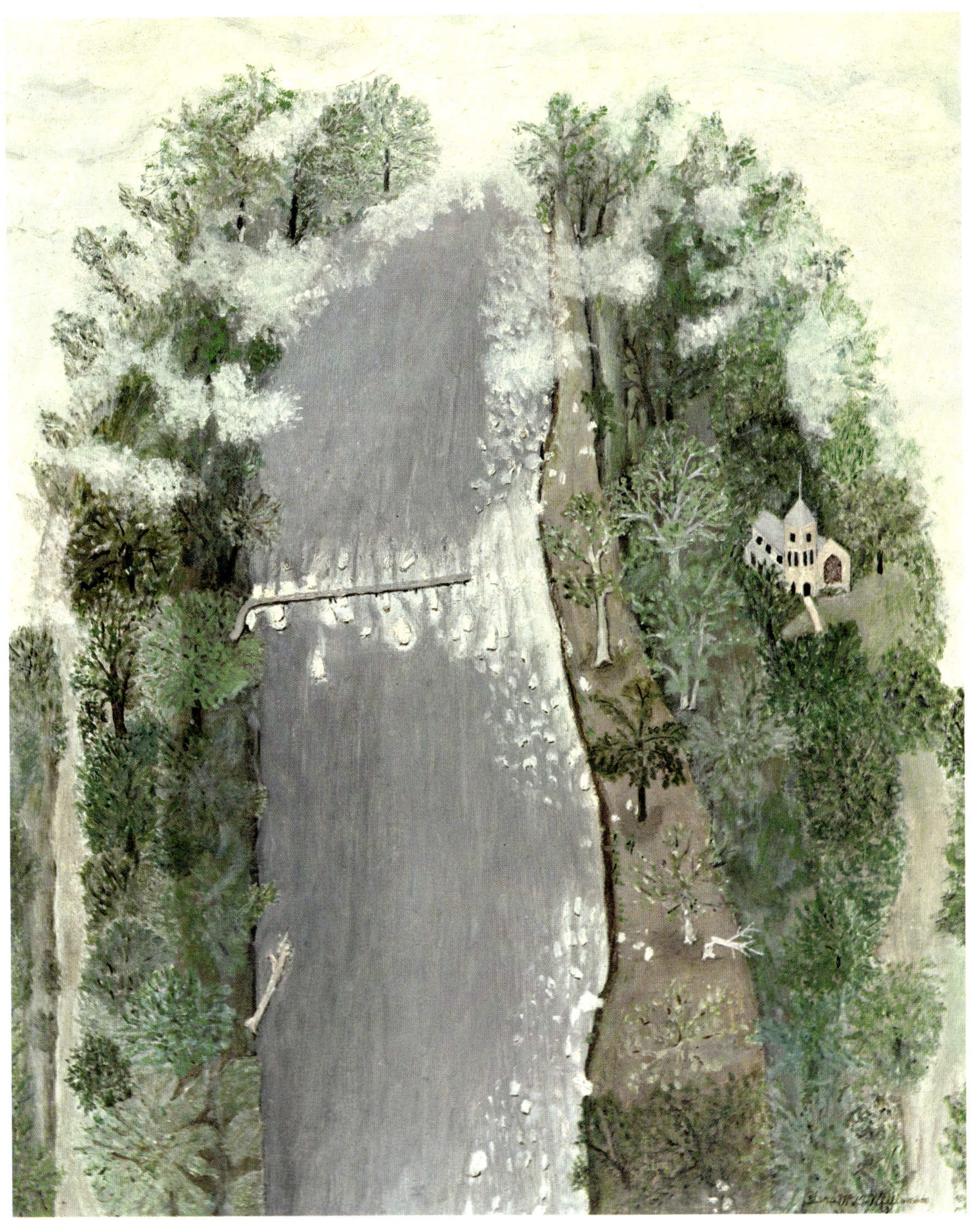

THE DREAM
Oil on panel, 1951, 25 x 21 in.; courtesy Mrs. Elizabeth Kennard, San Marcos

quietly and formally grouped; there is no tension, no real action. Only the boys scuffling in the water, and the splash and water movement indicating that a boy has just jumped in, disturb the strange formality of her composition. This, incidentally, is a painting that Aunt Clara "made" when she was invited (along with any other interested painter in the country) to participate in a competition sponsored by the Museum of Modern Arts, entitled, "The Human Figure," which may account for the static quality of the figures. It is particularly interesting to me, and was at the time she embarked on this subject for the competition, that she interpreted "The Human Figure" as pertaining only to the nude.

Paluxy Creek was such a charming and pretty place in which both children and adults might fish, play, or pass the time of day, that Aunt Clara, with many warm memories of it, has chosen to paint it twice, a rarity for her. And, as even rarer occurrence, she has painted this same location both in watercolor and in oil. The viewing angle and the detail are quite different, the varying mediums dictating oddly enough that the watercolor be more distinct in outline and more definitely stated than the oil with its delicacy and softness. The cabin on the hill, barely indicated in the oil, but stated log and stone in the watercolor, is the home of friend Gambler Tim Terrell, who left his pregnant wife and four children living there alone when Sneed shot him.

Fishing on the Duffau takes us to another favorite spot, which exists today very much as Aunt Clara has painted it from memory. It pictures the falls on the Duffau River just above the old iron railroad bridge, and just before the Duffau flows into the Bosque. The fishing was always excellent here, but the falls were most populated on Sunday afternoons when, there being little else to do in Iredell other than watch the train come in, the courting couples used to pair off and walk along the Bosque from town to the falls. There they would spend the better part of a Sunday afternoon, picking wild flowers from the meadows, strolling farther to meet and chat with other such couples, or sitting around talking, skipping stones in the pond above the falls and watching the water slip past to splash down over the rocks. It was a refreshing and cool respite from the weekday routines.

Clara was in her middle teens when the county finally built the bridge across the Bosque that figures so prominently in many of her

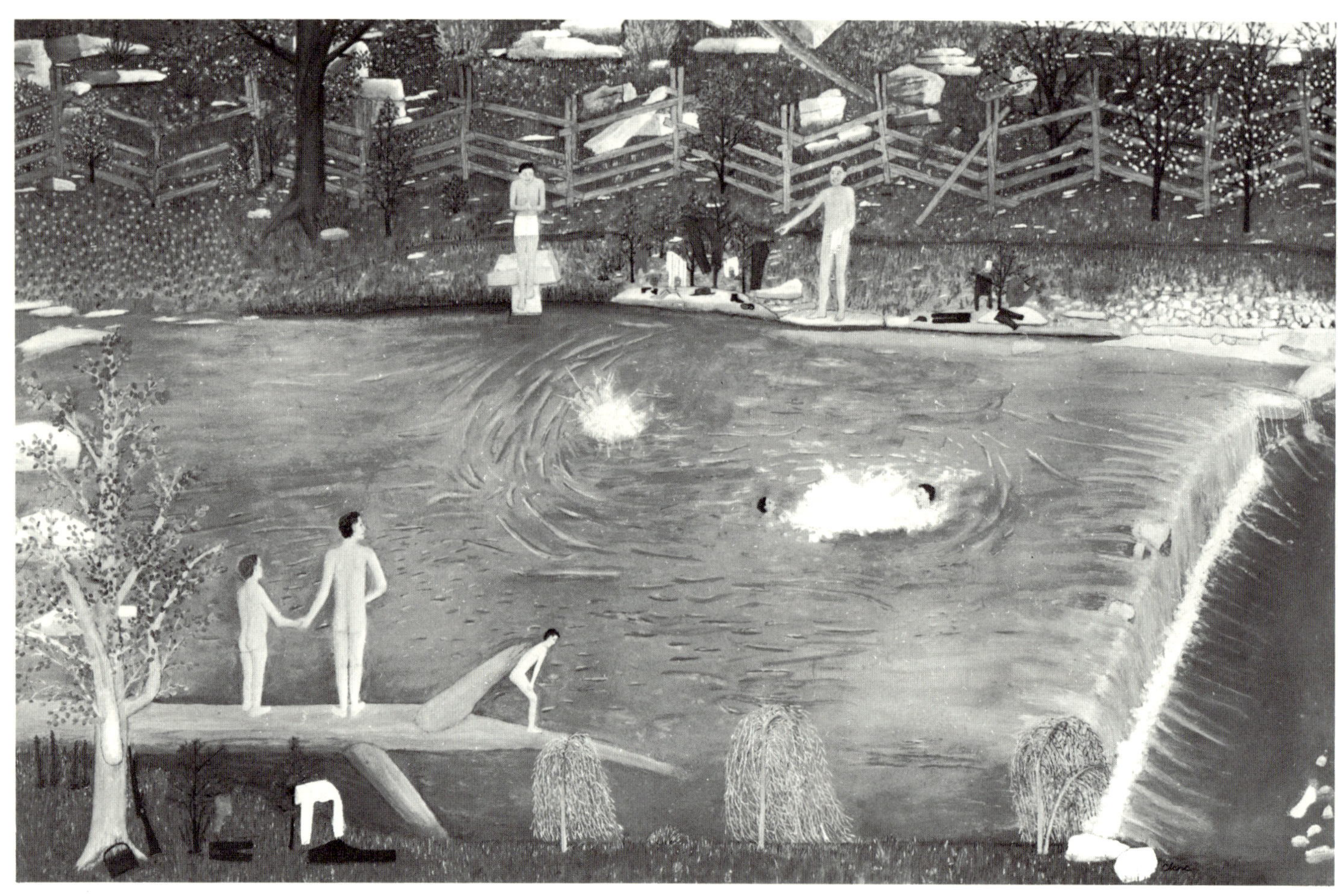

AT THE OLD SWIMMING HOLE
Oil on panel, 1960-1961, 24 x 38 in.; courtesy Valley House Gallery, Dallas

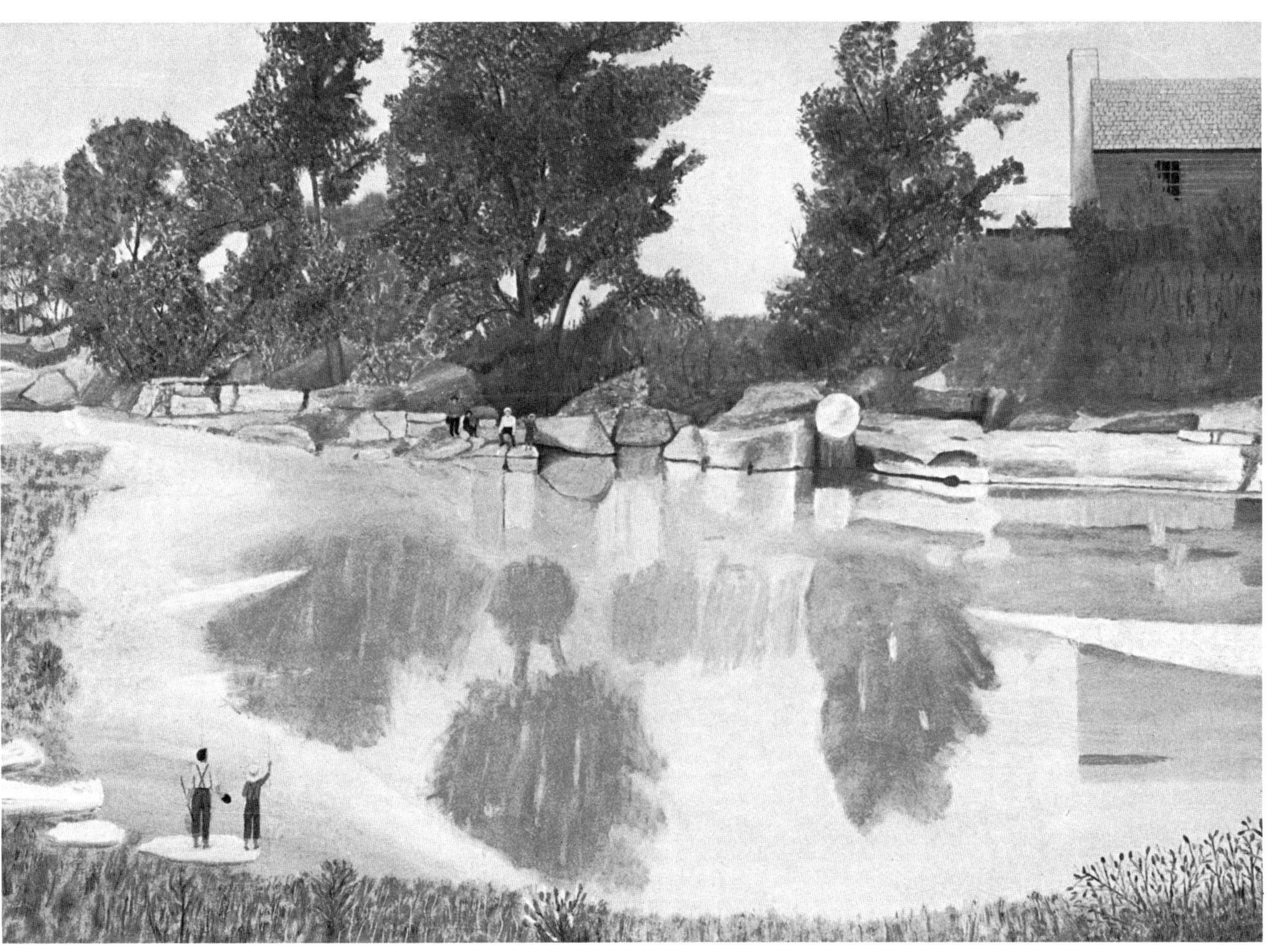

PALUXY CREEK
Oil on panel, 1956, 22 x 33½ in.; courtesy Miss Ann A. Lafferty, Dallas

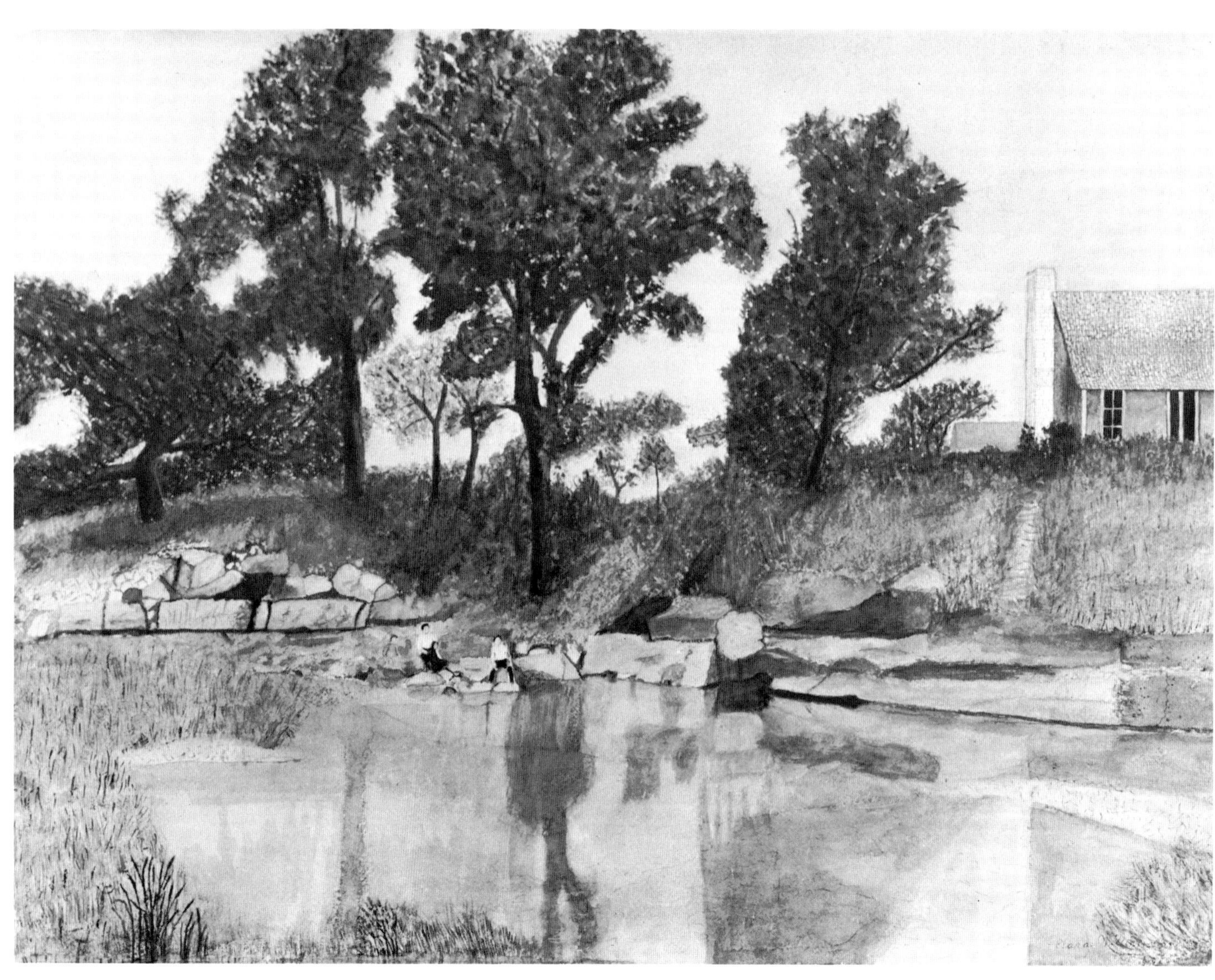

PALUXY CREEK: TRANQUILITY
Watercolor, 1946-1947, 17 x 23 in.; courtesy Mr. and Mrs. A. C. Swygard, Dallas

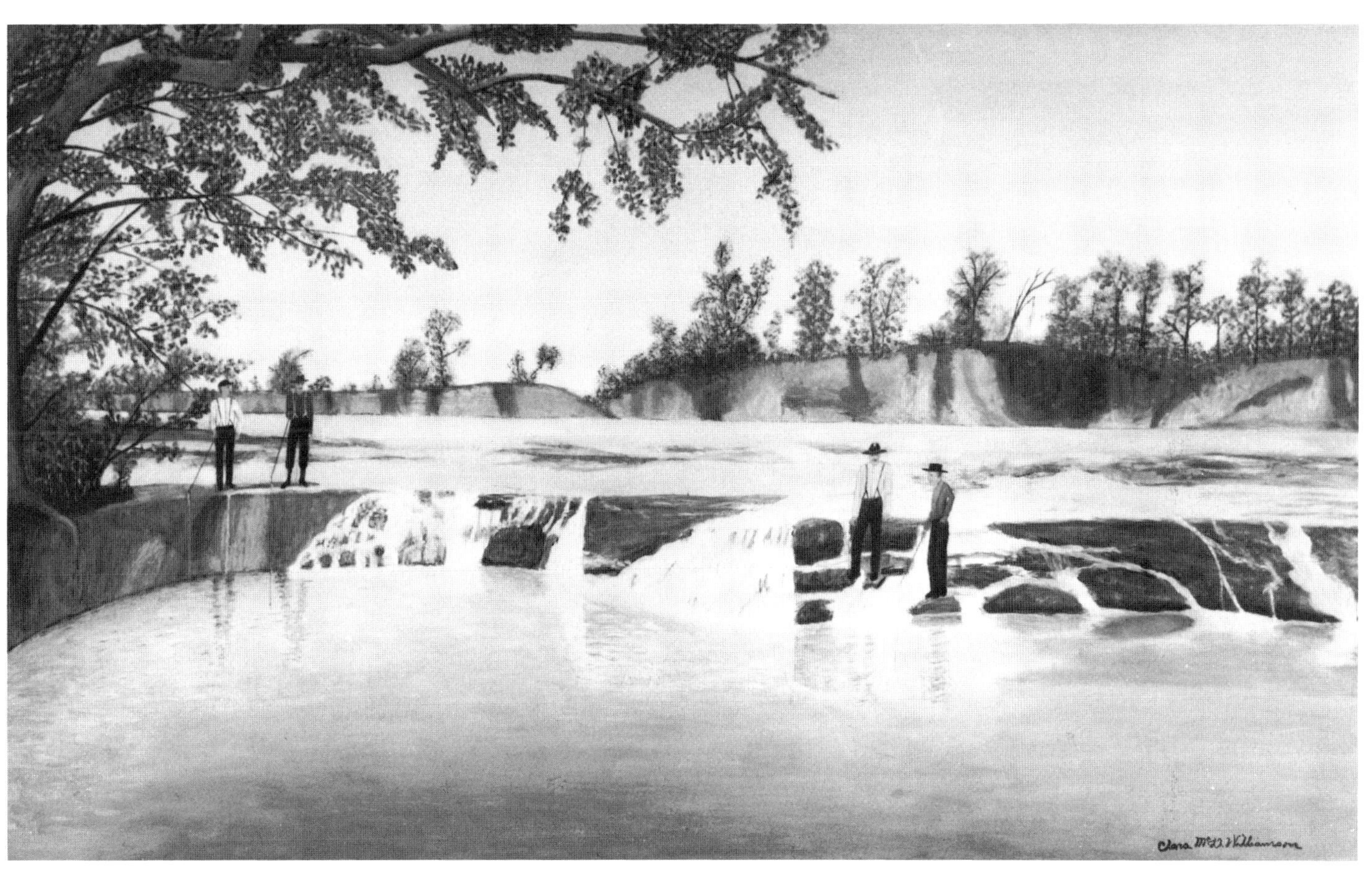

FISHING ON THE DUFFAU
Oil on panel, 1954, 18 x 30 in.; courtesy Mr. and Mrs. Denys R. Slater, Jr., Dallas

paintings. It was a country iron bridge, and gave good service, lasting until just a few years ago, when it was replaced by a flat, uninteresting concrete structure. And once the bridge was built there was no one in Iredell who did not wonder how they had managed without it, for it made the Bosque traversable in all seasons and weather, and welded the northside and southside communities into a closer relationship. It was so important — as a reference point, practically, and visually — that Aunt Clara painted *The Bridge, Iredell*, both in oil and in water-color, as she did Paluxy Creek. Both bridge pictures are quiet reflective paintings, and it might have been in reference to these that she spoke again one day about the need for painters to paint what they knew, and knew well.

"I wish I'd lived closer to the big waters, the Gulf or someplace — so I could paint some seascapes, you know. But I just don't know enough about water to undertake that. I know about little rivers — but you just can't succeed in writing or painting something you don't know."

The new bridge on the Bosque, besides being an all-weather crossing, became the starting point for the courting couples who walked on a Sunday to the Texas Central Railroad bridge and to the falls on the Duffau; it was a place for foolhardy youngsters to show their strength and prowess. Clara's older brother, Allen, who should have shown more restraint, since he was a cripple and had dragged his left foot since he first learned to walk, was one of the first to climb to the top of the bridge. And one moonlit night, on a dare, he walked clear across the river on the highest section of the bridge. Clara was terrified that he would fall, but even then seemed to understand that because her brother was a cripple he had to prove himself over and over.

Another night, when Allen was up the Duffau fishing with a friend, one of Texas' freak thunderstorms came up suddenly, and before the boys could reach the railroad bridge, the river had swollen to a fast torrent. By the time they were ready to cross the bridge the water had risen over the railroad tracks, and as they jumped to shore on the opposite side the bridge gave way and washed downriver to the Bosque. The boys arrived home to find a frantic mother and sister Clara awaiting them, but all they suffered physically from the experience was wet feet. On this occasion the new bridge over the Bosque stayed clear of the flooding waters, and little damage occurred in the community.

The Day the Bosque Froze Over, which in conversation with Aunt Clara is always subtitled "Winter on the Bosque," records one of the most pleasurable and exciting events in the early history of Iredell, and one in which the bridge is a featured player. The Bosque often froze, it is true, and no winter was so mild that there was no ice at all, but the day memorialized in this painting was the only time that anyone could remember that it was frozen solid enough to "drive a team of horses across." Even the most timid walked daringly across the river on the ice this day, and told the unbelievers about it later.

Time stops for a moment in this painting; the townsfolk are as frozen as the river waters. It is just at sunset, the sky is blushed with a pinky orange, silhouetting sharply the figures on the ice, and even more sharply, those on the bridge, and everyone holds his pose as if a photographer were present. Which, indeed, he was, and at this exact moment, so Aunt Clara tells me, had finished focusing his tripod-held box camera, and had said, "Now, just hold still until I say you can move."

I have seen the photograph that was taken that day; it is charming and very like the painting. But it lacks the atmosphere that Aunt Clara has created in her painting, where the cold, white sheen of the snow contrasts with the delicate coloring in the glow of the sunset that shades the sky with warmth. One of the many qualities that sets Clara Williamson apart as a naive painter is her masterly restraint in the handling of color and her perceptive use of the closest color values. It is most uncommon to find in her paintings a moment that is unharmonious, that "jumps out" at the viewer with raw color. The nicety of her treatment of a sunset, as in *The Day the Bosque Froze Over*, is an excellent example of this exceptional restraint and perception.

Aunt Clara's shared memories of the rivers and creeks of her childhood do not by any means exclude the land and its importance

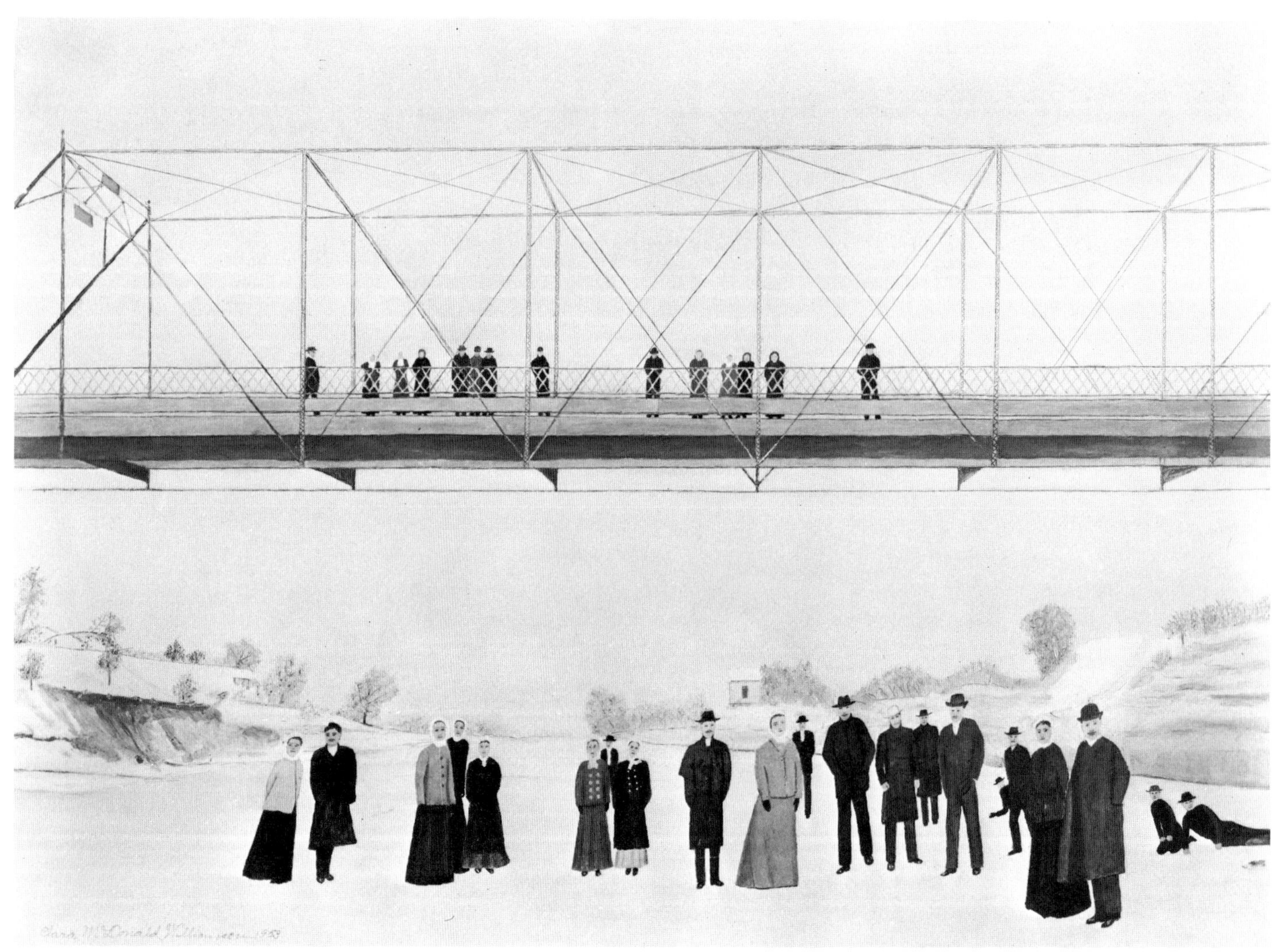

THE DAY THE BOSQUE FROZE OVER
Oil on panel, 1953, 20 x 28 in.; collection, The Museum of Modern Art, New York, New York. Gift of Albert Dorne.

in her early life. One of Clara's earliest and most persistent memories is of the garden her mother always planted and tended, in which she grew the better part of the family's year-round supply of fruits and vegetables. By careful rotation and staggered planting during the season of beans, peas, corn, and cabbage, Mary McDonald proudly kept fresh vegetables on her family's table longer than any other gardener in Iredell. And any surplus was picked when ripe and canned (jar upon jar neatly labeled and sparkling on the shelves when the cupboard doors were opened) for use during the off seasons, as well as for sharing with less green-thumbed neighbors. The picking fell mostly to the children, and was a chore that, for the most part, they enjoyed. Aunt Clara has not as yet painted her mother's carefully planned garden, but she has done a gay, tiny picture *of Aunt Fanny's Garden,* in which a sunbonneted lady tends a happily brilliant flower bed. And it can be assumed that Clara's mother dressed much as this when caring for her tender seedlings.

There is also a marvelously handled charcoal drawing (the only one extant that I know of), simply entitled *Man Plowing,* that portrays Uncle Joe guiding the plow behind a team of horses, while in the next pasture above, a tiny colt frisks in search of his mother. The subtleties of the gradations of the grays to blacks in this drawing, and the differentation texturally between the plowed land, the pasture land, and the hillside even to the sky, are quite remarkable. Charcoal is here employed as if it were her usual medium of expression, rather than one used only in an isolated instance.

In the early days Iredell was a cotton town, supporting at one time two cotton gins. Certain parcels of land throughout Bosque County and the neighboring counties were particularly rich in the kind of soil from which cotton grew in full, high stocks. One such parcel was the Walker Ranch, and in her teens Clara occasionally helped with the picking. Here the growth was so abundant that one hardly had to stoop to pick, and the usually back-breaking labor was considerably eased. At picking time the cotton wagons with their high, slatted sideboards were parked in the fields until full and brimming; then as they were hauled to the gin they left wind-blown, white shards in the grasses lining the lanes along their route. At the gin they lined up, wagon to wagon, awaiting their turn; there were so many to be unloaded at the height of the season.

In *Cotton-Picking Time* one moves down the rows with the pickers,

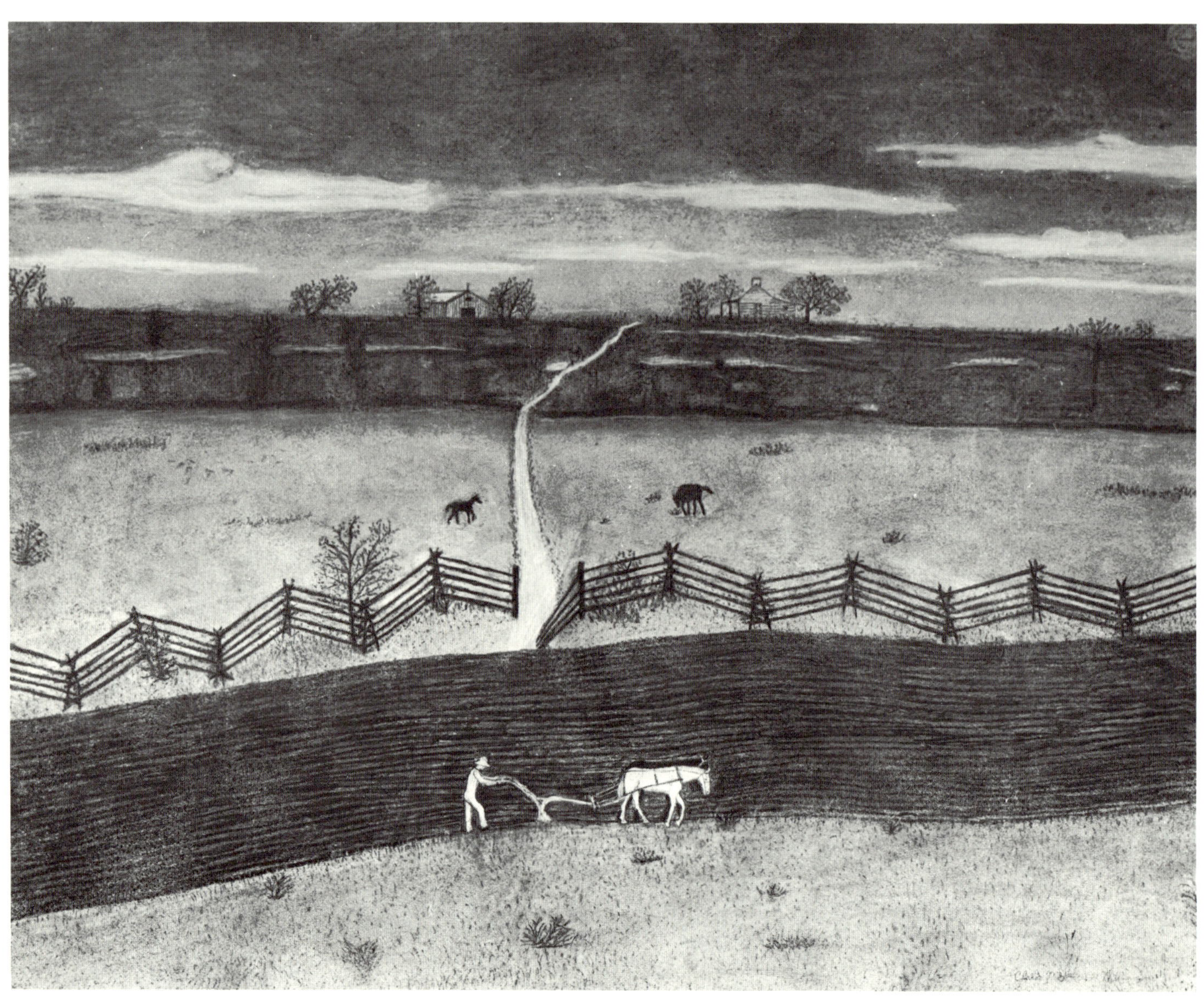

MAN PLOWING
Charcoal, 1946, 23 x 29 in.; courtesy Mrs. Tom Beckett, Jr., New Hope

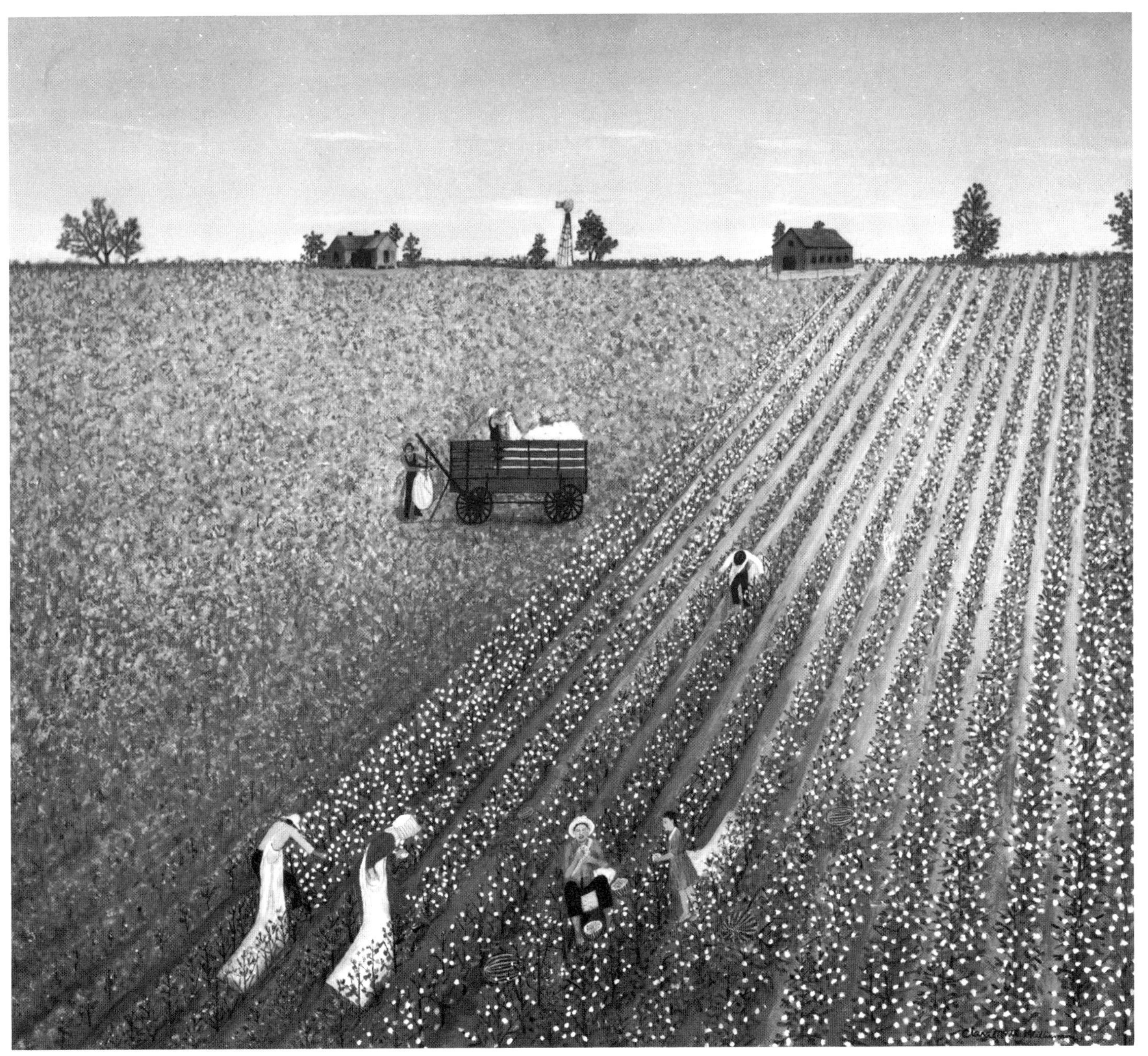

COTTON-PICKING TIME
Oil on panel, 1952-1953, 24 x 27 in.; courtesy Texas Bank & Trust Company, Dallas

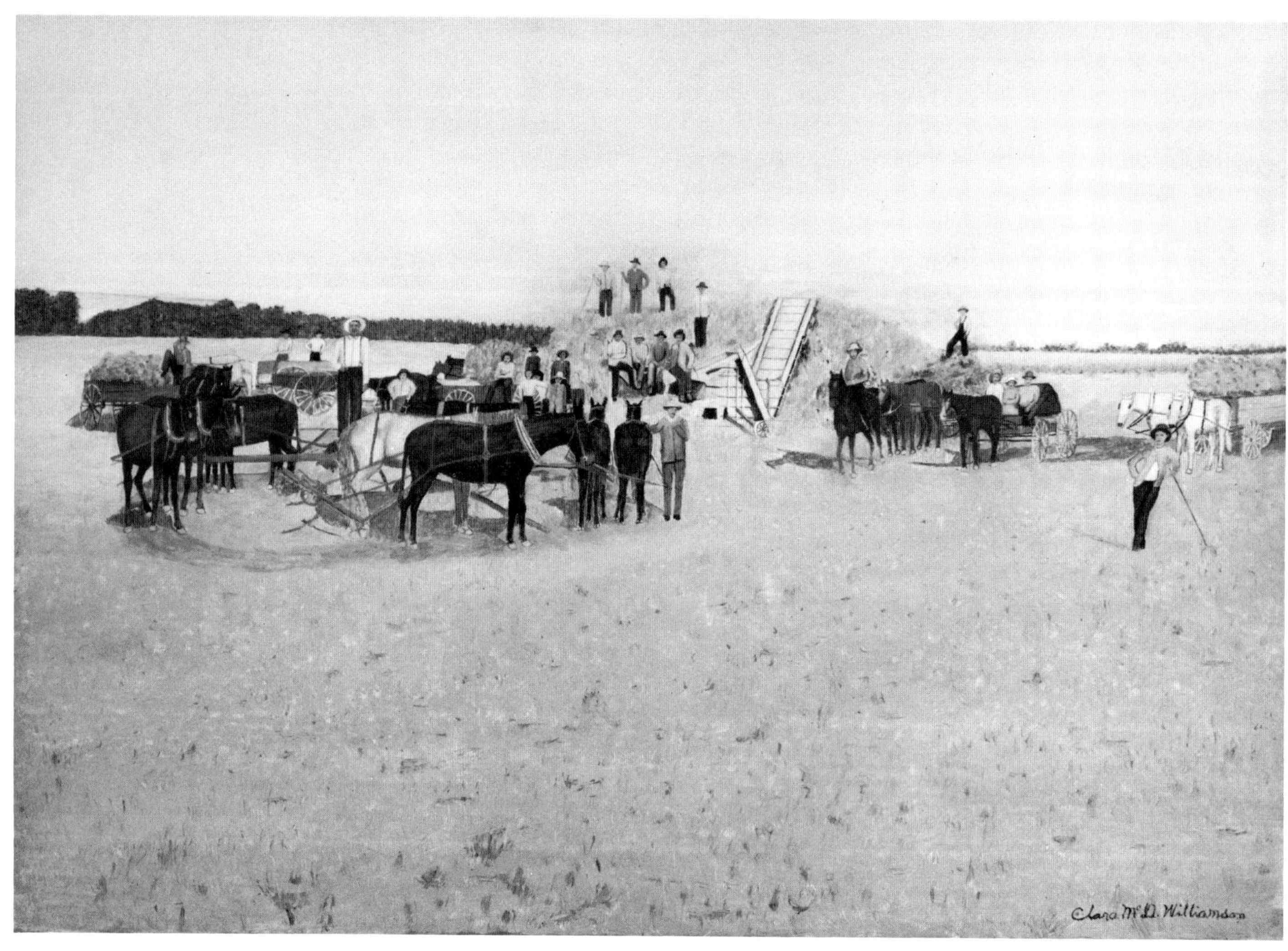

THE HARVEST
Oil on panel, 1954, 20½ x 28¼ in.; courtesy The Stewart Company, Dallas

long white bag trailing behind, marveling at the fullness of the cotton on the stalk, and feeling the heat and the crick developing in the bent back. One is dulled by the monotony of the picked-over field to the left, and the steady, never-ending rows of cotton to the right, then refreshed by the sight of an occasional watermelon breaking the regularity of the rows, and by the man who sits enjoying the juicy pink flesh of one as he rests on half-full bag of cotton. The house and barn and promise of shelter from the hot sun are distant; to reach these havens, more cotton must be bagged, then unloaded into the wagon. It is hot and still, and the day promises to be long.

But the monetary rewards were ample, often great, even for those who did not plant and pick the cotton itself. Clara's father traveled a good deal during this period of her life, building cottonseed-oil mills up into North Texas and even as far north as Arkansas. He was his own architect as well as builder, designing as he built with the plans forming in his mind. It was not only such mills that he was commissioned to build, but fine, large frame houses that spread out and around, and sometimes even boasted two stories. He was much in demand, still being, at that time, the only well-known carpenter in the area.

And there were of course many crops other than cotton, primarily grain, that were planted to nourish life, both human and animal. Since planting season was pretty much the same for all the farmers and ranchers in the country, harvest time, too, came to all at once, when the Texas sun ripened the grains and turned the fields to gold. Then the neighbors would band together, and taking their teams, wagons, and threshing machines, go from one man's fields to the next, until all the rich harvest had been brought in.

In *The Harvest* Aunt Clara has once again, as *The Day the Bosque Froze Over,* leaned on a photograph for inspiration and a nudge of memory. This particular harvest occurred in Blackstock Valley, a very rich section in the northern part of Bosque County, at Grandmother Henderson's prairie farm. The threshing is going well, and the pause is for the photographer and posterity, if not to catch a collective breath. Mr. Jim Harris is driving the mules, and a couple of the Simpson boys are in the picture; those in the buggy just drove out to see the men working and to add a bit of encouragement.

No photograph was involved or needed in *Harvest Hands at Dinner;* it is a scene in which the young Clara participated quite often, helping

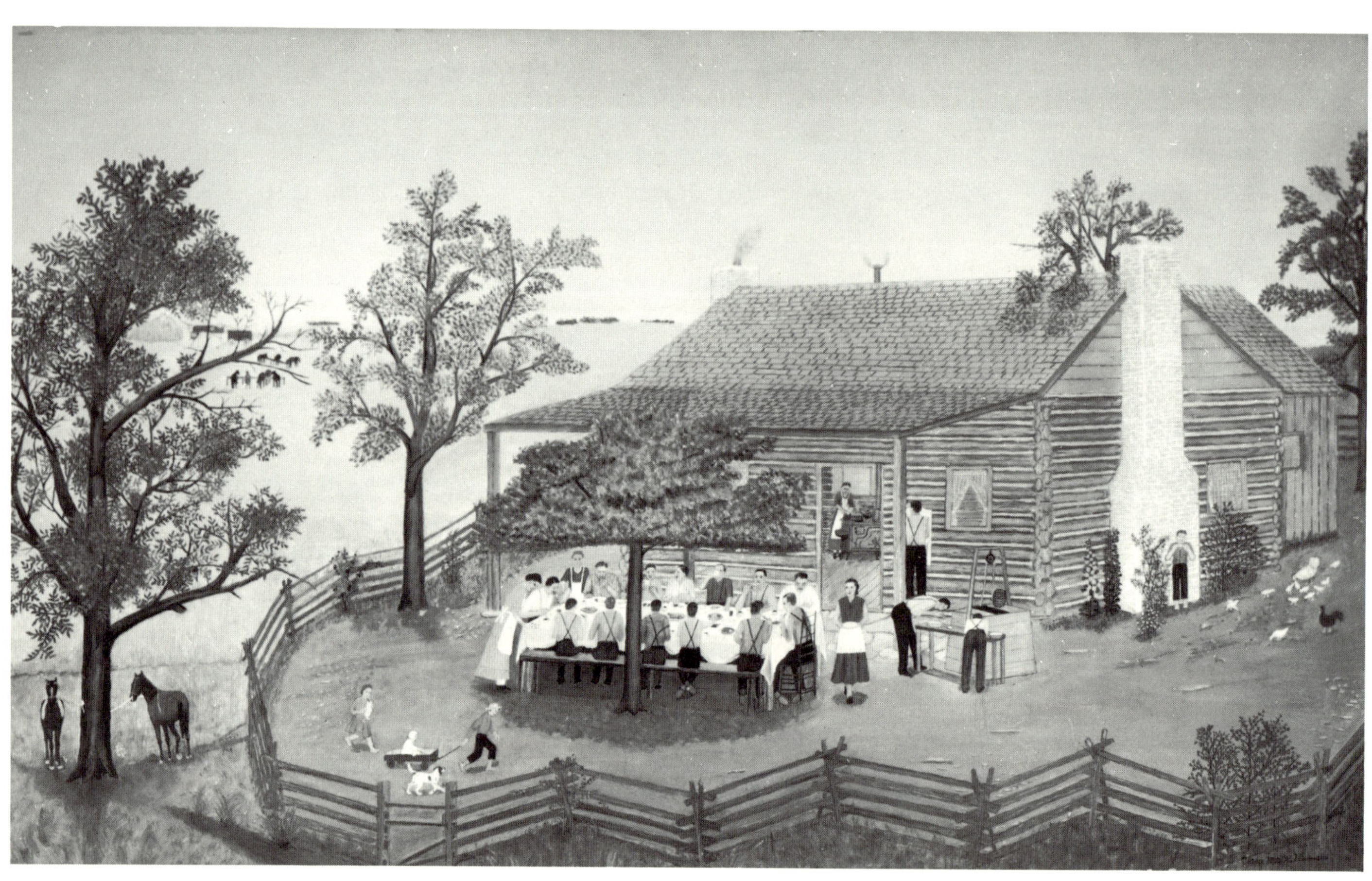

HARVEST HANDS AT DINNER
Oil on panel, 1953, 24 x 40 in.; courtesy Mrs. Amelia Anderson Fuller, Dallas

out a relative or a neighbor during the harvest season. The men have come in from the work in the fields for the midday repast, and, after a quick wash-up at the pump, settle wearily in the cool shade of the flatly spreading tree at what amounts to a makeshift banquet table, an actual "groaning board." The kitchen is obviously too small for such a huge table, and since during this season the weather is predictably hot and dry except for an occasional vagrant thundershower, there is little risk of a rain-spoiled meal.

The family whose fields are being harvested supply the food; the womenfolk cooking and serving until the men can eat no more. It is a festive time, and all is friendly banter and good will and neighborly joshing; and once again an opportunity for the young men of a family to become better acquainted with the young ladies of another. Even if talk at table is seemingly relegated to subjects of interest only to the male, there is also much less obvious interplay between server and served. When the men have finished, the women and children will sit down for their bite to eat and a rest in the breeze-cooled shade, before clearing and returning to the hot kitchen to prepare the evening meal. In the painting one half-grown youth, his hunger too strong to postpone appeasement, has stolen an ear of corn and gone around the side of the house to hide by the chimney and probably to burn his tongue in his haste to finish his prize before he is caught and chastised. It must have seemed to the women that in diverting their energies from the usual routines and rechanneling them for the short period of the harvest to catering on a large scale they became suddenly, though briefly, purveyors to an army.

Another painting seems to have a natural place in a discussion of the land, and that is *The Produce Man's Visit*. The peddlers, such as the produce man, came through the town from early spring, through the summer, into fall; in the winter, the roads being more difficult, they were not seen in Iredell. They brought with them, besides seasonable produce, the storied wares of the peddlers of the west: from needles and threads to heavy cooking utensils, piece goods, and the staples — flour, sugar, and coffee. Before stores were opened in a pioneer town these men with their full wagons were the only source of dry-goods items for the settlers, and often remained so, particularly for those who settled far out and for whom a monthly trip into a town was a rare occasion. Wherever he went the peddler was also a source of news and gossip, and usually found everywhere a warm

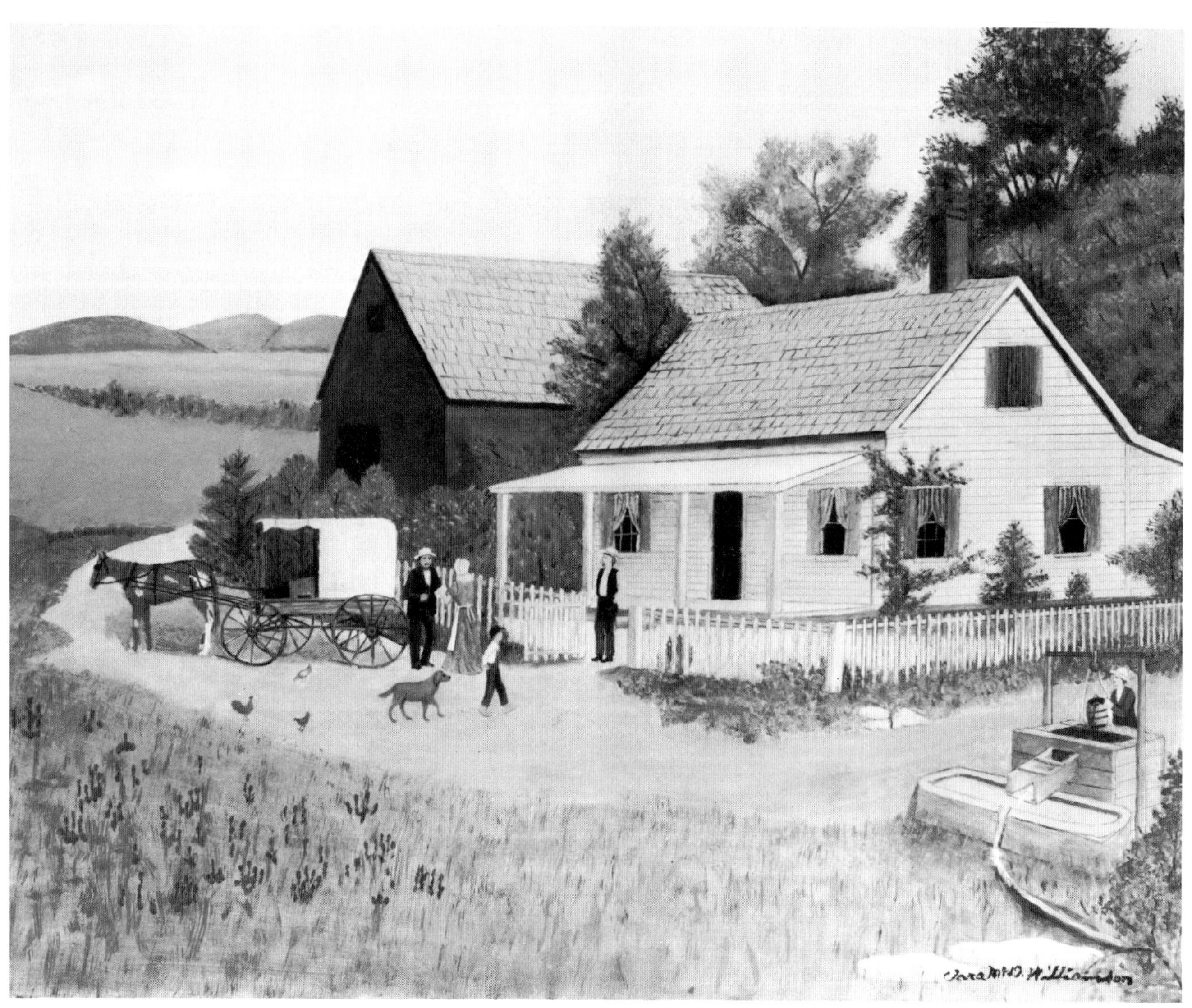

THE PRODUCE MAN'S VISIT
Oil on panel, 1954, 15½ x 19½ in.; courtesy Mrs. Elizabeth Kennard, San Marcos

greeting and an eager audience for both his wares and his tales. However, in one instance, this was not the case.

A peddler called one day at the home of Clara's Aunt Laura Williamson. She took time from her work to look over his wares, as he pressed her to do. But after inspecting what he had to offer, she decided that she didn't need anything that day, and bid him goodbye. At this rebuff the peddler became very angry and most insistent that she purchase something. Aunt Laura was home alone, the men being out in the fields, so she just stepped inside the house and got the shotgun down and, pointing it firmly at the peddler, told him that if he didn't pack up and leave she'd shoot him. It is perhaps unnecessary to add that he left.

I n *Village on the Bosque, 1890* we are once more invited to the McDonald Place, this time to stand at the front gate, toward the edge of the bluff, to look out again to the farthest boundary of Clara's world, where the spur of the Davis Mountains almost becomes a part of the sky. It gives one the feeling of being on the top in a game of "King of the Mountain"; one so surely rules with pride the toy world below.

The boys have ridden up the hill to do a little courting; sister Addie has blossomed in her early teens and become sought after by the young men in Iredell, so the boys have come to show off a bit with their rope tricks and horseback riding. Addie and her brother stand by the opening in the red fence and watch, teasing back and forth with the boys; they have but to lift their eyes to see what Clara saw, beyond, in the valley.

The panorama is quite differently presented here than in *Chicken for Dinner,* where the activity in the foreground is made so interesting that attention is held concentrated there. But in this painting, one can not long resist looking beyond the performing boys to the enchantment of the valley below, and the myriad activities occurring down in the town and all around the countryside. Once in the valley, one is

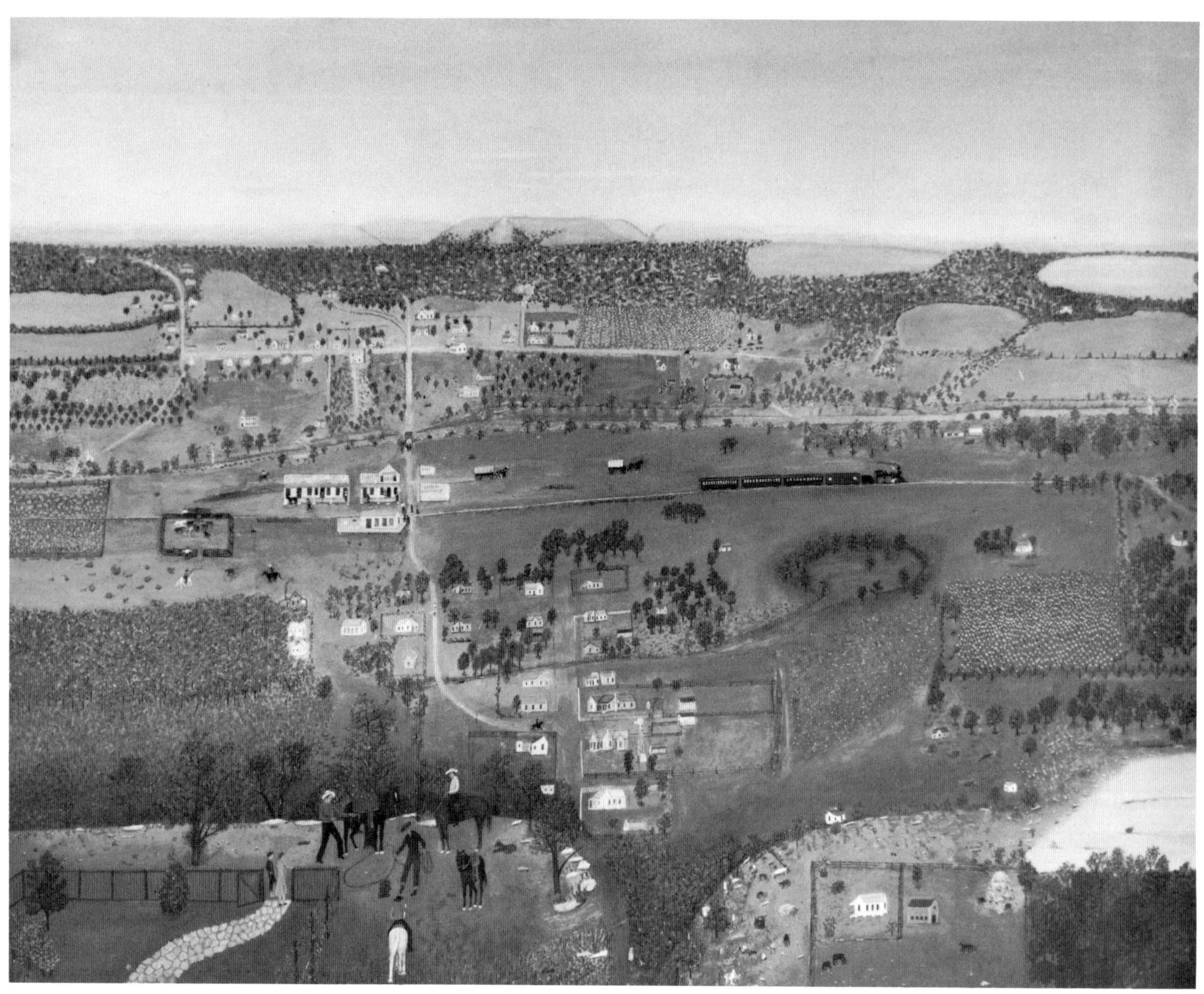

VILLAGE ON THE BOSQUE, 1890
Oil on panel, 1959, 38 x 48 in.; courtesy Mr. and Mrs. John L. Paxton, Fort Worth

permitted to explore at one's own pace the delicacies spread out in such tempting array, and make the many discoveries Aunt Clara has prepared. I do not wish to discuss this painting in detail, feeling that it is more rewarding here for the viewer to roam and wander at will through the landscape as proffered.

As minor orientation, however, it may be said that the viewer is looking from north to south, and the train is moving to the west. In 1890 Clara would have been fifteen, and in this painting, and in actual time, the bridge which one sees crossing the Bosque had just been built. But the village of Iredell, which she pictures here on the north side of the river, as it existed when she was very young, had by this time been washed away by the flood and rebuilt across the river, between the bridge and the crossroads one can see just beyond, on the south side of the river. So actually, this is the whole community of Iredell as it existed before the flood, with the exception of the bridge.

One can identify the Methodist church of *Arbor Meeting* just across the river and to the left of town. Children are running toward it as if they are late to school. To the right of the crossroads beyond the bridge is the Baptist church, and next to that, still to the right, between the road and the river, is the town cemetery, as it was then and can be found today.

Village on the Bosque is a patchwork quilt of a painting, each piece worked in loving detail, then fitted carefully into the marvelous design of the whole. It is a visual delight as an intricately patterned whole, and in each "piece" held in the quilting frame, wherein one enjoys the liveliness of this village of Iredell.

When the leaves all around the county had just changed color, and a certain crispness was felt in the air, it was time for the last big get-together before winter set in. This fall gathering was never held in Iredell itself; it always took place some distance away, at a particularly pretty spot in the countryside that was convenient for the townsfolk as well as those from the ranches around, just far enough to make it a change and a bit of an adventure.

The one we visit with Aunt Clara, in a painting she calls *Autumn Outing,* was held at Glen Rose Spring, one of the loveliest in Somervell County. It was a big church picnic, and gathered here were not only family groups from farther around than one can see, but almost more different conveyances than were found in *Arbor Meeting.* When

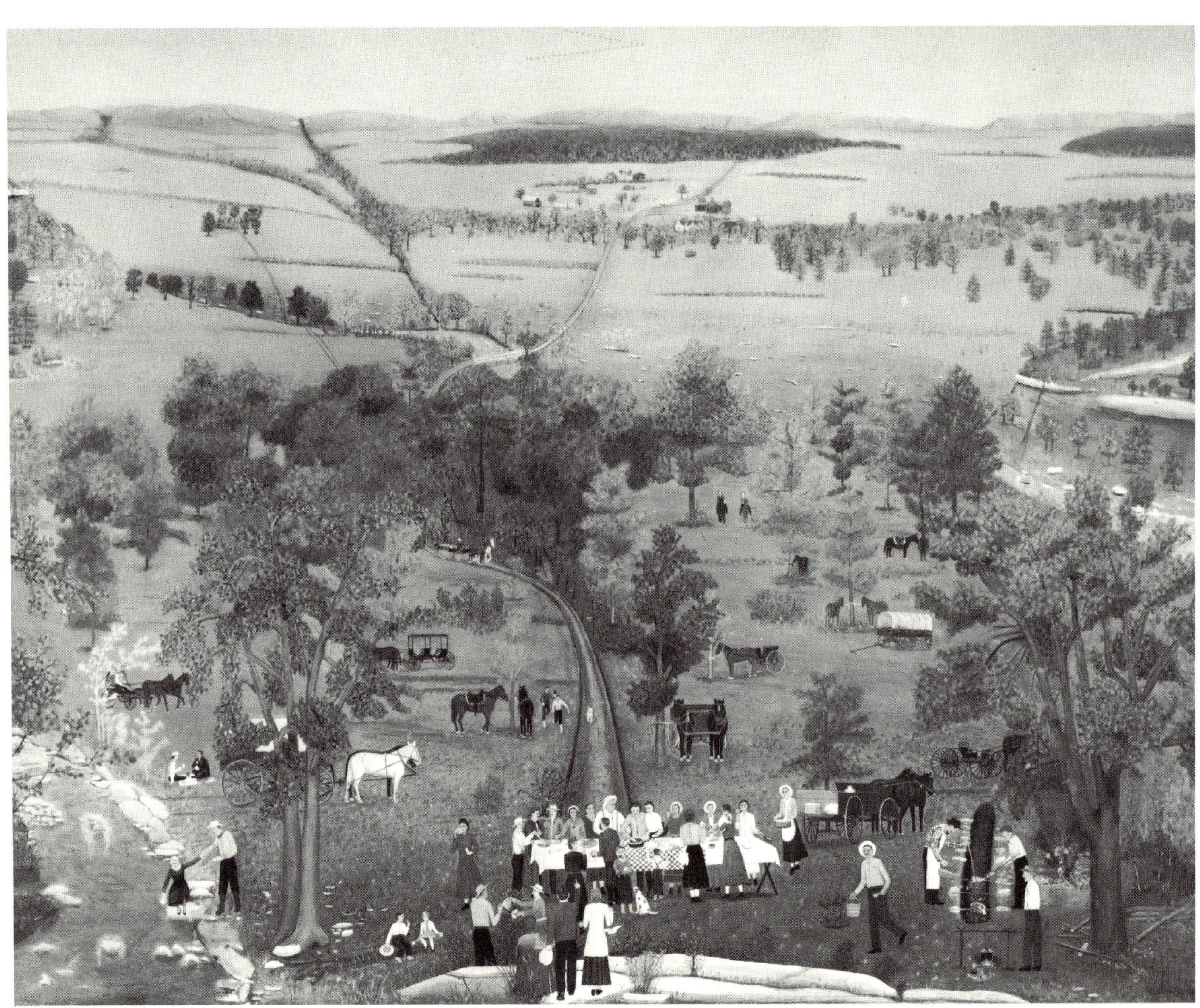

AUTUMN OUTING
Oil on panel, 1951-1952, 48 x 60 in.; courtesy Mr. and Mrs. Waldo Stewart, Dallas

I asked if there really were such a variety of rigs at this picnic she answered that sometimes there were, and that there might have been, and besides, "it makes it more interesting that way."

For such a special occasion a fattened beef was killed, and the mystic preparations involved in a full-scale barbecue were undertaken. Grandfather Lasswell was an authority on how to barbecue beef properly, and on this occasion, it was his advice that was sought, as was so often the case. The procedure was to dig a trench, such as that seen to the lower right in the painting, which was filled with hot coals. Across the trench were laid fresh-cut green branches to support the meat, and atop these were placed the skewered slabs of beef. These were turned at specified intervals, hot coals were renewed as needed in the trench, and sauce was daubed on the cooking meat from time to time. The smell of this half-roasted, half-smoked beef as it slowly reached the exact stage of perfection, sniffed in the cool, fall-scented air, was almost more than the hungry young could bear. It can be seen that a few of them, and adults, too, could not wait, and started in on the other picnic provisions brought by the ladies' guild before the beef was ready.

After the feasting, on these occasions, music always followed. Often selections would be played by a brass band that Dr. Wysong, one of the preachers, put together, but when the band didn't materialize, there was always singing — rousing happy singing on a full stomach in full voice. All of the favorite church hymns were sung, usually including "In the Sweet Bye and Bye"; it wasn't until the long, sleepy ride home to the rhythm of the hoofbeats of the horses that the music might change to a popular tune of the day — a love song, perhaps, or a lullaby.

Autumn Outing is another of Clara Williamson's truly exceptional paintings. The viewer becomes one with the couple standing on the huge, rounded white stones in the lower foreground, first surveying the picnic table, then moving down the gently curving trail and slowly across the richly multicolored fall countryside to the very top of the picture, where the vee of the wild geese flying south, both stops the viewer and returns him to the earth beneath and further visual wandering. The compositional keys to this painting are the vee and the gently curving arc. These two linear devices, and the forms they create, are repeated over and over throughout the canvas, interlocking these areas securely within the rectangle; each curve ending in a vee to begin another curve. An unbelievable organization exists in this masterwork, giving it a plastic quality that a fully sophisticated painter could not fail to admire and even envy.

As Clara grew through her late teens to her twentieth birthday not spoken for, and not even being "waited on" by any special young man, she gradually became more and more actively unhappy. The girls were spoken for early and married young in those days, and a maiden of twenty with no immediate prospects was considered an old maid, so much so that when the children started referring to Clara as "Miss Clara," the final seal was put on her supposed spinsterhood.

It is to be assumed, of course, that Clara had as little time free to make herself available for courting as she had had as a child for the schooling she wished for so desperately, or even the time to become a capable organist, as her sister had. The matter of the organ being just one more example of her restricted life, for when her mother was at last able to swap a horse for a long-awaited little reed organ (something for which Clara had yearned from the first time she heard one), Clara was a "grown girl," and as she puts it, "Well, my sister younger than I and I just ate that organ up, we loved it so. She could play better than I could, she had more *time* to play. Well, you see how limited my opportunities were and how handicapped I was, but I don't look back."

She might well have been speaking of her lack of opportunity and freedom to participate in the courting rituals of the day. She was much too busy being her mother's reliable and needed helper, and working, always working, doing housework, cooking, and looking after the younger children in the family. Certainly she must have longed, as she grew to womanhood, to exchange this work in her family home for that in a home of her own. She adored her younger brother and sisters, and really did not mind in the least caring for them, but they were not her own children, although they must have often seemed as such.

It is little wonder that when Clara's Uncle Allen Lasswell, who was the County Clerk of Ellis County, with offices in the courthouse at Waxahachie, invited her to move to Waxahachie and work for him,

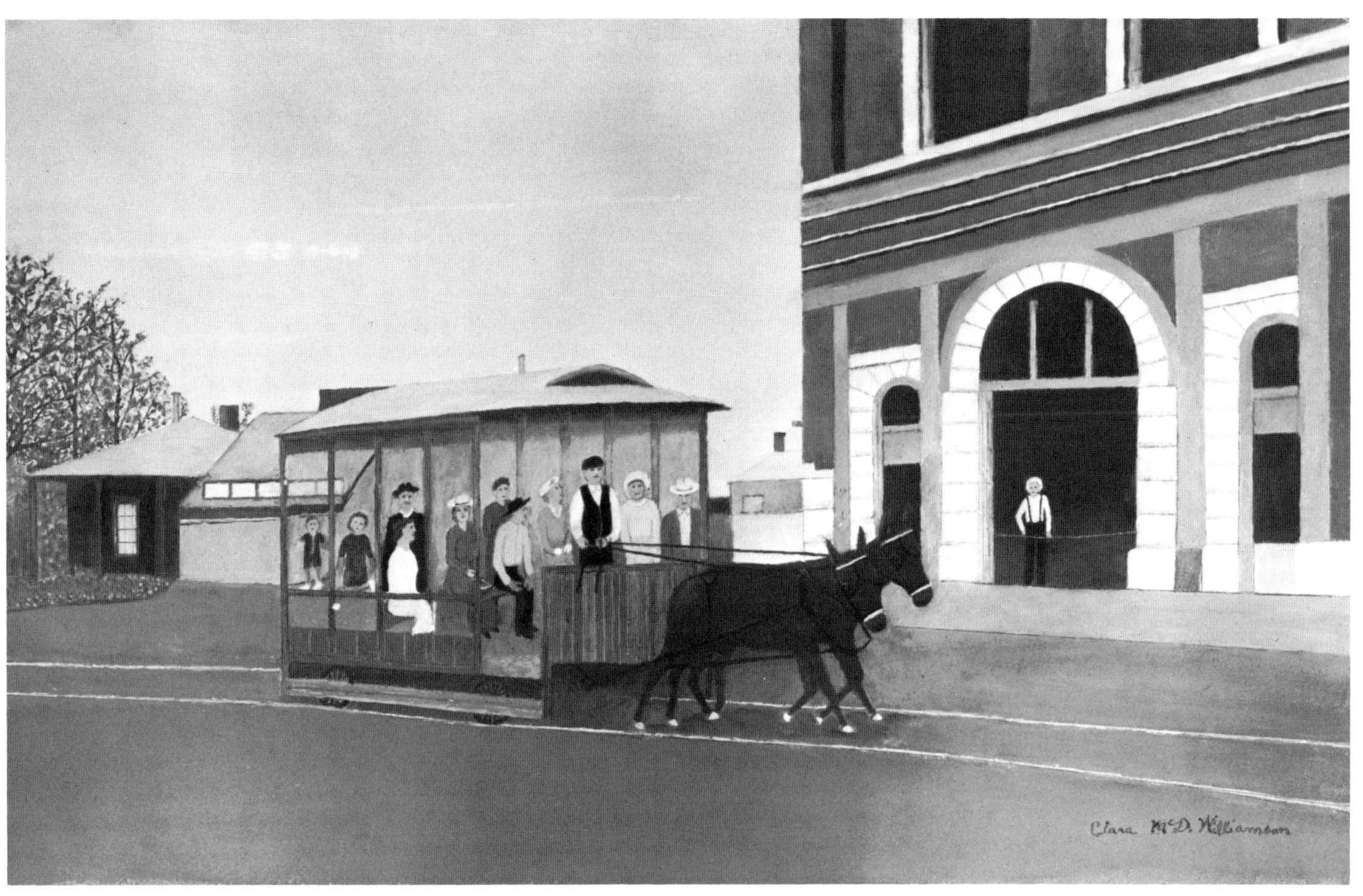

STREETCAR, WAXAHACHIE
Oil on panel, 1964, 15 x 24 in.; courtesy Valley House Gallery, Dallas

it was without hestitation that she agreed to go. It was escape from an intolerable situation that held little or no promise.

She spoke of it to me in this manner, giving her warm chuckle as she said, "You never saw a poorer, more ignorant, greener, country girl go up to a big town than I was when I went to Waxahachie — it was pitiful. I'd lived there in Iredell all my life and just worked at home and helped my mother with my brothers and sisters and this and the other, and all the time I was unhappy. I was very ambitious and I wanted to learn to do something, even longed for it.

"A lot of people can look back to their early days and say, 'Oh, the good old days!' But *I* don't wish I were back there again — not me! But oh, how I loved to do the office work once I got on to it! You know, I had never even seen a typewriter, or anything — but it wasn't more than a couple of months till I was making the transcriptions. I just loved it — I had the most pride in it!"

This was a happy life, and the years that the emancipated Clara spent in Waxahachie are remembered only with the greatest pleasure on her part. She loves to speak of them, and tells all sorts of delightful anecdotes about her life as an office worker, her fellow workers, and her friends. This was indeed the life of the emancipated woman, and one that Clara was not long to catch on to and enjoy. It was a world in which one worked from eight or nine o'clock until five, and then was free to do as one wished to do. There was enough salary, small though it was, to take care of room and board and send a bit home, and even save a bit, and time outside of the office was leisure time. There was time to read, to walk, to think, to learn, to do anything one wished, with no demands other than what one placed on oneself.

Of course, the demands Clara placed upon herself were always stringent. Her aims and ambitions being high, she hated to waste any time that could be used in learning or doing. But since this was carried on in an atmosphere of warm comradeship, it seemed more like play than work. Primarily, it was freedom to do what she wanted to do. The lawyers, court officials, all the men who were in and out of the courthouse, could not help but like this eager, earnest young woman, who tried to so hard to please and was so quick to learn. They quickly came to call her, not "Miss Clara," but an affectionate and comradely, "Miss Mac," a title she cherished. She might have known nothing of office work when she arrived in Waxahachie, but she took to it like the duck to water, and she was soon an expert.

She tells an amusing story about learning to type. It seems there was only one typewriter in the courthouse, which was presided over by a young lady a bit Clara's senior, who typed all the court work. She evidently became a little jealous of Clara, because the latter, a new-comer, was immediately liked and accepted, and even the young men were quite respectful and kind to her. Miss Lizzie, the lady in question, did not receive this same respect, and was called "Liz" to her face to tease her, because she was so high-strung and her temper so easily aroused.

When Miss Lizzie went to have her dinner in the middle of the day, Clara would immediately sit down at the typewriter and practice until it was time for Miss Lizzie to return, going without her own lunch in her eagerness to master the machine. When Liz realized what her "rival" was up to she was just jealous and touchy enough to play a mean trick on Clara. So just before she left for her dinner each day she rolled a form with several carbons into the typewriter and did a bit of typing on it. She left this in the machine when she went to dinner. And as Aunt Clara says, "You know, you just can't roll back a piece of work with a carbon copy in it." So there Clara would sit, staring with frustration at the machine. When one of the young men finally noticed her there and asked her what the trouble was, the ensuing conversation took place:

"Well, Miss Lizzie's left her work in the typewriter, and I can't type or practice today."

"Well," he says, "why don't you just roll it out?"

"Why, I couldn't do that!"

"If Liz did that just for the heck of it to bother you, *I* can do it," and he walked over there and rolled it out.

"I said, 'Now listen, don't make her think I did that.' And he said, 'I'll tell her who did it, don't you mind'."

"And when Miss Lizzie came back and started yelling because her work was ruined by having been rolled out of the typewriter, he peered around the corner and told her to stop blaming me, that he had done it. Well, she just went wild and started throwing books and everything at him. He ran to the circular staircase and poked his head out from time to time, and each time she saw his head poke out, she threw something at him. Law, it was the funniest thing you ever saw!"

And Miss Lizzie left no more carbons in the typewriter, and Clara readily perfected her technique, and soon was taking dictation from the lawyers on the typewriter, and doing all their copying for them. Actually, she first started sketching during these years in the courthouse, for in working for the courts, she had to copy land sketches to the transcripts and court records from little scraps of paper that men drew on in the country, and brought in to have recorded. Some of the notes on these were in Spanish, and as she says, "I didn't understand them, but I made accurate copies."

One of her greatest rewards came on the day the lawyers for whom she had been working all got together and presented her with a new typewriter, to be used in place of the old Oliver. "Oh, I did love that work!" she says, over and over. It was so very satisfying to be relied upon for new skills that had been acquired through her independent efforts, that she had learned because she *wanted* to learn them.

It was indeed such a uniformly happy and pleasant period of her life that we have only one painting as a record of those seven years or so. There was not just *one* good moment among the bad to be remembered and painted across a span of seventy years or more as there had been in her childhood; this was such a generally rewarding period that few occasions stood out as happy landmarks.

Actually, there might be no paintings to remind one of this time if I hadn't happened to ask her one day, out of curiosity, if they hadn't had those mule-drawn streetcars when she lived in Waxahachie, and she had said that they did, and that she always felt sorry for those little mules pulling those heavy full cars. And so she painted *Streetcar, Waxahachie,* to show me how it was, with a firehouse behind the streetcar to indicate what a big city was the town of Waxahachie.

After around seven years of most satisfactory existence in Waxahachie, the enriched and emancipated Clara McDonald, because of an Ellis County political upset, suddenly returned to her family's home in Iredell. Nothing there had been changed and no one accepted the fact that this was a different Clara who came back to her home town; no one realized that this was "Miss Mac." She was promptly, though unwillingly, absorbed into the household duties as if she had never left, and into the life of the community, where "Miss Clara" was now the settled form of address to this obviously confirmed spinster.

In Iredell, however, was a fairly recently widowed gentleman, around ten years older than Clara, who was not put off by the community's pliant acquiescence in that young woman's spinsterhood. He had been left with two small children to raise, and had of necessity temporarily placed them with his wife's father (old Brother Roberts), but the little boy, who was near seven, was proving quite a handful, and the grandparents were having a hard time with him. So John Pierce Williamson was looking for a wife; one who was not too young and flighty; one who was used to bringing up children and working hard; one who might be eager to marry and not too particular about the fact that the husband came supplied with a family. Surely, Clara McDonald was just such a one. But it wasn't to be as easy a conquest as he thought.

John Williamson, though born in Mississippi, had grown up in a tiny place northeast of Iredell, called (because it was) Rocky. He was left an orphan at the age of twelve, and had further misfortune of shortly thereafter acquiring as a stepfather "the meanest man the good Lord ever let live — a man by the name of Renfro." The boy spent as little time at home as possible, for an immediate and violent hatred developed between him and this man his stepmother had married. His chief outlet for dispersing this violence and energy was to ride horseback — to ride fast and hard on the wildest ponies he and his friend, Ed Greer, could find. His ten-year seniority over Clara meant that he had spent his early childhood in an even less civilized West: one where the horses were wilder, the settlers sparser, and the Indian raids more frequent.

John's friend, the already-mentioned Ed Greer, was famous throughout the area as the hero of one of these raids. One evening when Ed was still very small his grandmother chanced to look from the window and see a group of Indians sneaking up on their cabin. The two of them were alone there, the old woman and the boy, and there was no help within miles. As darkness slowly obscured the shape of objects outside, Ed's grandmother scurried him out to the gatepost of the fence in front of the cabin, sat him on top of it, and tied him there. As the Indians grew bolder in the darkness and came closer, the terrified boy on the gatepost became to them, in silhouette, a man, and they rode off to harass a less-protected family. The grandmother became well-known throughout the community for her cleverness in having saved the family goods and perhaps the boy's life and her own, but Aunt Clara, in telling of this, said, "I just couldn't have put that little boy on that gatepost."

But toughness was necessary for survival, and John Williamson grew up tough, and self-sufficient. An uncle had a combination grocery and hardware store in early Iredell, and he wasn't doing too well with it. He was an excellent persuader, if a poor businessman, and talked young John into investing in the failing business, which promptly began to prosper.

John, reared there in West Texas, brought up on a farm, quickly became a well-thought-of merchant, a full and sustaining member of the Iredell community. He was a pillar of the Baptist church; he was a laborer for eternal grace; and he made a good living from the store, so was also a good provider.

But to Clara, when he came calling on her, he was in the same graceless state in which she had been prior to her move to Waxahachie; he had lived all his life in the little town of Iredell and its environs. And this didn't make him unhappy; he enjoyed the life of the Iredell community and, certainly during the period of their courtship, had no desire to change what was for him a most satisfactory environment.

Between these two, there was a difference that remained irreconcilable throughout their life together, and this stemmed from the religious convictions of each. John was a practicing Baptist and, as we have noted earlier, Clara was a Methodist, and, although Mama taught her children to be righteous and didn't just "teach them church," Clara suddenly became very firm about being a Methodist. She decided that if Methodism was good enough for her adored Mama, it was good enough for her, and when John tried during their brief courtship to persuade her to become a Baptist, she quite flatly refused. This was a tiny freehold she established before she would consent to be his wife, one she kept in independence and sometimes blatant revolution, throughout their life together.

In spite of their disparate religions and personalities, John and Clara reconciled enough of their surface differences to make the decision to become man and wife. There was much to move Clara into this marriage: the two motherless children who needed her love and help so badly; a home in which she would be the mistress; perhaps even the longed-for babies of her own; and certainly a vastly improved position in the community, as the wife of a respected merchant. It is not hard to envision the balance-scale tilting toward this union in Clara's mind, in spite of her many justified qualms.

The wedding took place in 1903, at the McDonald Place — the house on the hill. And after the ceremony Clara and John Williamson went down the hill into the north valley of the Bosque and into his home. It was close to where his children were living, so they simply stepped over and brought them home, too — little Faye, a charming girl of three, and the seven-year-old, the boy, John — and Clara began her married life.

T he duties that Clara promptly took up in her new home were little different from the ones she had left behind, with the addition of two new and vital roles: those of wife and mother.

The conquest of little Faye was an easy one for the warm-hearted Clara. Her affectionate and natural manner with the small girl brought a ready response; the child was only three, and eagerly accepted the security offered in motherly love and a settled household. With the boy, whom they called by his initial, "J," the conquest proved more difficult. This was in large part due to John Williamson's handling of the rebellious boy, which was stern and disciplinary. Clara was in the unfortunate position of trying to maintain the father's authority even though she often disagreed with his use of it, and at the same time, trying to win the boy's confidence, friendship, and trust. It is remarkable that she achieved this as rapidly as she did, for it wasn't really so long before "J," too, was running to her for understanding, solace, and affection.

The children also turned to Clara for explanations; another of John's tenets being that one never explained anything to children. He told them only what he wished them to know, not what they might ask or wish to learn. Clara's thinking ran along quite opposite

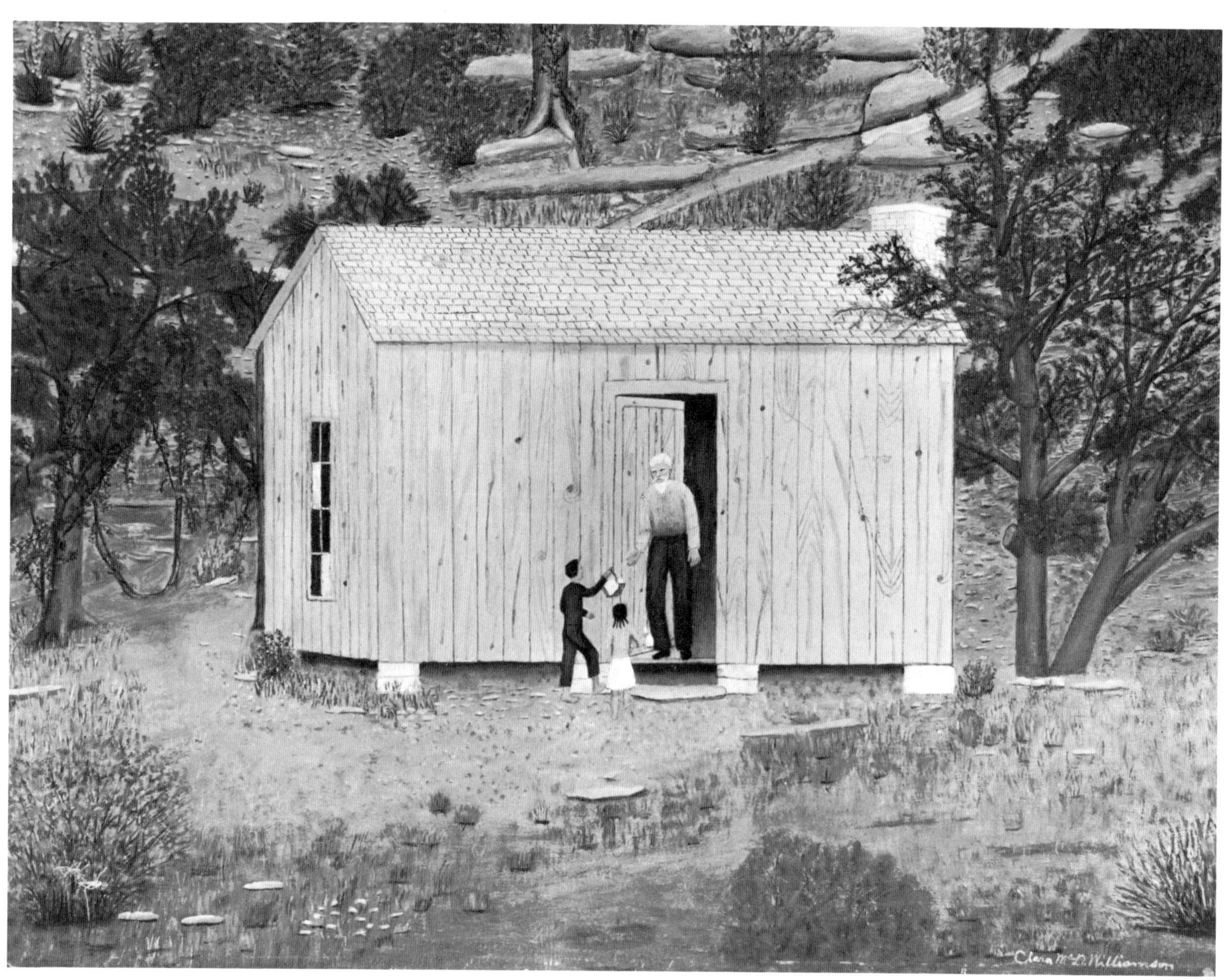

PAPPY CRONE'S CABIN
Oil on panel, 1955-1956, 18 x 24 in.; courtesy Mr. and Mrs. A. R. Frank, Grapevine

lines. So she gave the children as much time as she could manage to set aside for them during that first year of her marriage — answering their questions about anything and everything, stimulating them to further questioning, and seeking with them a basis for an enduring relationship of love and understanding.

She has painted one picture that shows "J" and Faye not long after they became her family. They are seen taking food to old Pappy Crone, who lived halfway up the hill we have become so well-acquainted with, in a cabin he built for himself of "boxing lumber." *Pappy Crone's Cabin* was a poor shelter (although it looks sturdy enough in the painting), but Crone was a rockmason, not a carpenter, and he lived by himself and had no one to care that it was not a fine house. He built fireplaces and chimneys around Iredell, specializing in the selection and laying of fine hearthstones. These he often decorated in most handsome manner and they were known to last for years and years, to the pride of the homeowner. This was a gentle man, and the children loved him and felt sorry for him, living alone as he did. Whenever their stepmother cooked something they felt was particularly delicious, they begged to take a bit to Pappy Crone, and Clara usually let them. The grapevine swing, temptingly placed near the cabin, was an added attraction, to be sure, but it is in the thoughtful act of giving that Aunt Clara catches the children in this painting.

In the summer of 1905, her only child was born, a son, whom she named Pierce McDonald Williamson, and called Donald. This was *her* child, and she lavished on him a concentrated love and devotion. The other children she had hoped to add to her family never came into being; so Donald received whole the attention that might have been divided among them. There was no lessening in her love for her stepchildren, or in her care of them, after Donald's birth; but raising them was much like raising her brothers and sisters before them; a slight objectivity could remain in their relationship, close though it was. They were not, quite simply, *her* own children.

These years of Clara's absorption with the children and household were active ones for John. He sold the grocery store, tried his hand at farming for a year, then when Donald was almost ready to start to school, he decided, with Clara, that they would open a dry-goods store.

Clara was soon at work in the dry-goods store at John's side, although one might well think her sufficiently burdened before adding this new role. This new part of her life gave her a lift, a bit of the

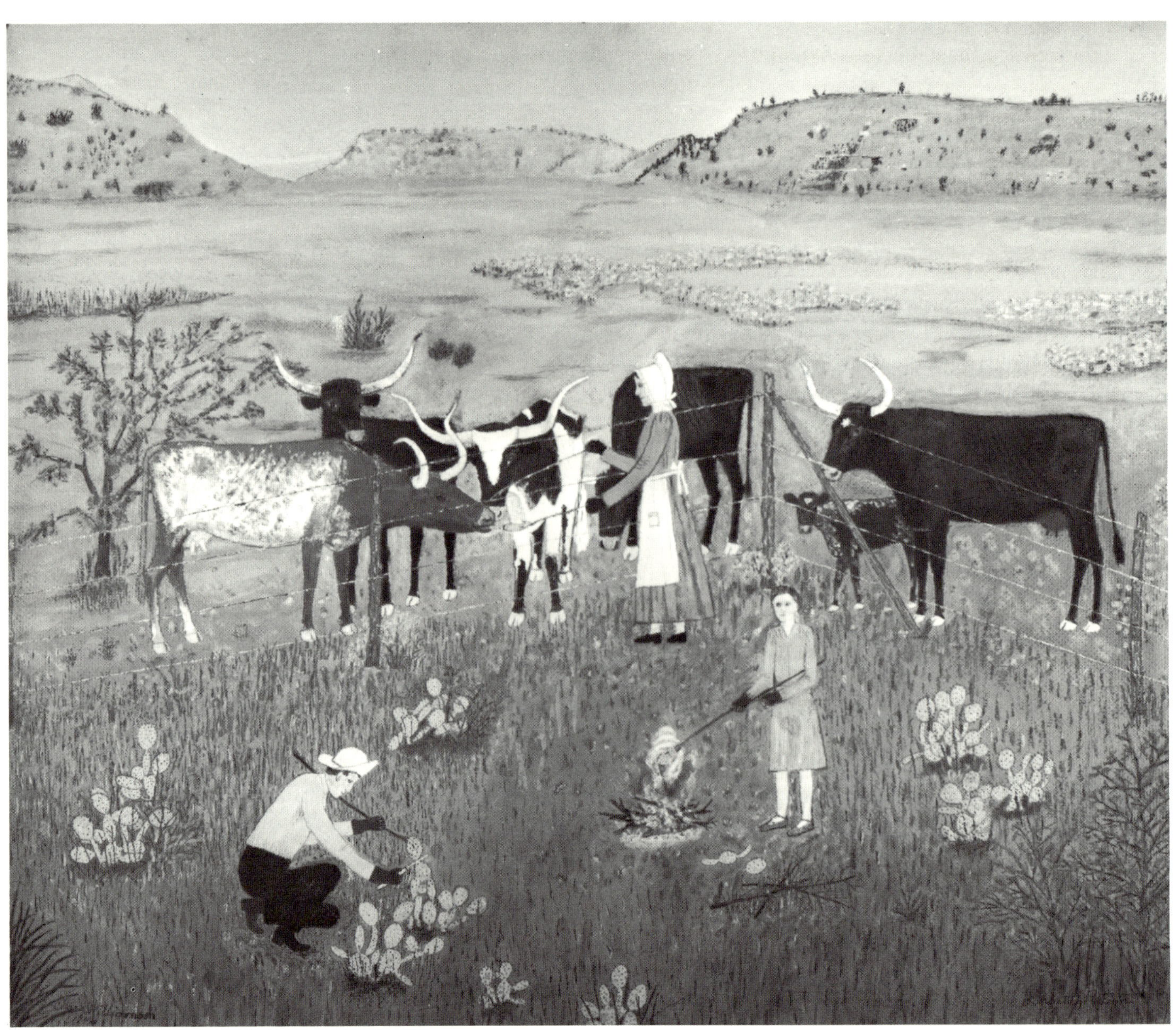

DROUGHT RATION
Oil on panel, 1946-1947, 20 x 24⅛ in.; courtesy Washington Art Galleries, Miami Beach, Florida

feeling of the days in Waxahachie, but it had to be tucked in around the other necessary work: the cooking, the washing and ironing, the sewing and mending, the cleaning, and the care of the children. One wonders that she found a moment to spend in sleep, for there were also the diverse church activities to fit in, and some social entertainments and gatherings outside of the church.

She kept Donald with her constantly when he was tiny. Her little son was not permitted far from her side; she wished to bring him up herself with vigilance and care. As with the other two children, she always took the time to explain things to him, to talk to him, to share her learning and experience with him. Primarily, as he grew, she worked to encourage the curiosity and hunger for learning she seemed to feel in him, much as she had felt it as a child. And this boy was not to be handicapped and frustrated in his desires for an education as she had been. All three Williamson children were sent to school as faithfully and religiously as to church; no chore or work was important enough to keep a child from school.

During a brief period in their marriage John and Clara drew very close, and forgot their differences, even those of religion, for a common goal. In this they were joined by the whole of Iredell, for it was a time of severe drought, and the common goal was rain. Aunt Clara remembers only one other drought experienced in Iredell that might be comparable, and that occurred when she was a girl, and one she pictorialized in the painting *Drought Ration*. This shows a family burning the spines off the cactus so as to feed and water their starving, thirsty cattle, to keep them alive a little longer. An unusual communication of sadness comes from this picture, of almost hopelessness, in spite of the life-giving actions occurring; it arises from the combining of the dryness of the land, the caved-in boniness of the cattle, the heat from the fire merging with the parched heat from the land and withered grasses, and the cloudless sky. It invites participation in the rescue, but does not completely promise that rescue will be also salvation. Although the mood here is oddly unresolved, and perhaps in this sense not representative, *Drought Ration* still ranks with Aunt Clara's best pictures; it is so beautifully designed and painted.

It could well be representative of the bad drought of which we speak; the stock were dying all around on the ranches; the Bosque and other rivers and creeks had dried to small, evaporating pools; the land baked into great, gaping cracks; and still no rain eased the mounting fears and tensions. The drought grew so crucial that the preachers started calling prayer meetings, so that the power of prayer could be put to work to call forth rain.

At first these meetings were held quite separately, the Methodists in their church and the Baptists in theirs, but as conditions worsened it was felt that by joining forces, by joining the congregations of all the churches, more power might be generated, and the drought broken. As it happened, on the first night of this joint experiment Clara went with John to the Baptist church, and she knelt there with him in his church, and they stayed there all night until sunup. They would sing a while, pray a while, nod a bit, and go back to singing and praying again. There came a tiny cloud in the sky, but to the north it was still the driest sky ever seen.

The next night they went to pray again for rain, this time at the Methodist church. "And do you know," says Aunt Clara, "it rained on us on the way in! And we went on into the church together and laid down every little prejudice we ever had, and knelt there, Methodist and Baptist, in prayer. Nearly everyone in Iredell was there praying together. And that night it really came down — it rained and rained till you couldn't see out! And you know I had to laugh that it was the praying in my church that finally broke that awful drought!"

With the continuance of the rain and the end of the drought the congregations separated once more, and although Clara and John had enjoyed this joint communion together in the Lord's Houses, they both remained hardheaded, and each returned to his own church. And the Williamson household, along with many others in Iredell, went back to a relieved normalcy.

As the years passed many changes came to Clara's world, but they were only the natural ones that might be expected with growth and the passage of time. Her beloved father and mother had sold the McDonald Place on the hill shortly after her marriage, and moved to Dublin, Texas; John and Clara made a move from the north to the south side of the river, to be closer to both school and store; the three Williamson children grew faster than one could keep track of, as children do; and the business prospered.

The store became more and more a source of interest to Clara, as well as of continual hard work, and she constantly sought and found new outlets and ideas to stimulate the prosperous business. At one time she began designing and making hats for the ladies of Iredell, having found none in the catalogues that she felt were pretty enough to order, and this quickly became such a successful facet of the business that she had to give it up, for it took too much of her time. She ordered from Dallas some of the very first "ready-to-wear" dresses, but was still so wary of their possible success that she took them only on consignment and wouldn't buy them until they also had proved successful.

Two delightful paintings, both done in the last several years, tell of one unusual and wonderful afternoon that broke the seeming sameness of these years for Clara. It was so exciting that it took two paintings to tell of it, for in this one afternoon she went for her *First Automobile Ride* and saw her first airplane. This latter picture carries the long title of *Transportation, the Old and the New, circa 1919, Meridian, Texas,* which gives fair notice that by the time she painted this particular "scene," Aunt Clara was most aware of being a "recorder of Texas history" as well as recorder of her own exciting experience.

This is what she told me of how this outing came about:

"I was married and working in the store there in town, you know, and William Schenk came along and said he was going to drive along down to Meridian. It was about eighteen miles of road; it was crooked, then, down to the county seat. He said, 'You know, there's a fellow coming in there in a plane, an airplane, and I want to see the thing. You want to come?' And John says, 'No, I don't care much about going; maybe they'll have some more of them later, and I can see them then.' And William turned to me (he'd known me all his life) and said, 'Clara, why don't you come and go.' I said, 'Well, I don't know, I hadn't thought about going.' And John, he turned around and he said, 'Well, if you want to go down there and see it, why you go

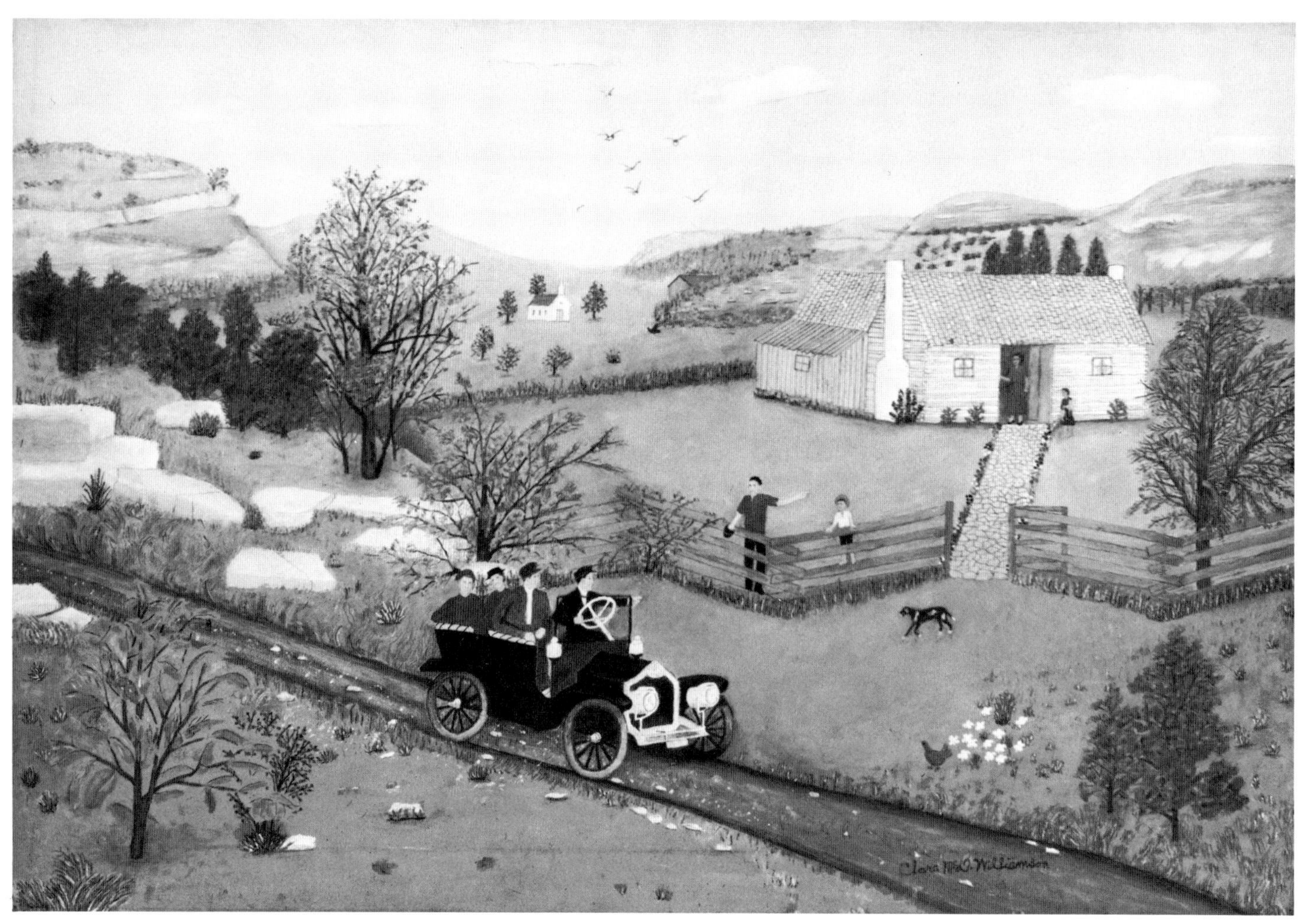

FIRST AUTOMOBILE RIDE
Oil on canvas, 1962, 20 x 30 in.; courtesy Dr. and Mrs. Earl L. Carter, Dallas

with William.' (We always called him William.) And I said, 'Well, I believe I will!' (We had two girls to wait on the customers in the store just then.) And I did."

Her holiday is as refreshing for us now as it must have been for her on that day. In *First Automobile Ride* she is seen in the back seat of the splendid auto as they motor along the roundabout route to Meridian. They have paused for a moment to ask directions and perhaps to show off the car a bit, and it can be seen that the noisy automobile is still enough of a curiosity to bring the man and the boy to the fence, and the woman to the door of her house; the dog barks in agitation; and the hen has hastily gathered her chicks to the side of the road. Aunt Clara shows us a time when the car had won partial acceptance, but retained the excitement and fascination of a novelty.

Transportation, the Old and the New . . . portrays the group after their arrival in Meridian. Aunt Clara has given her friends and herself a change of costume; this is a different painting and a different story. The other belonged to the automobile; this (although the auto and its accouterments are indeed present) belongs to the plane and to the wonder of man's flight.

Quite a small crowd has gathered to view the marvel, as this is not only the first airplane that Clara had seen, but also the first airplane seen in all of Bosque County. The plane is just about to land, and, with those who watch from their vantage point in the painting, we hold our collective breaths to ensure a safe return to earth. The children, who have stayed in the field looking up at the landing plane until the last possible second, race to the safety of the grove of trees. All are dazzled by the airy and fragile quality of this machine with its frail, whirling propeller, and cannot but compare it with the sturdy and accustomed heaviness of the steadily chugging train crossing the bridge in the background. Aunt Clara has caught and held for us, with capable hand, the breathless magic of such a moment.

When I saw this painting for the first time, at Aunt Clara's invitation, I could only exclaim in delight, and immediately settle down for a pleasant and rewarding exploration of the canvas. After I had spent a little time with the picture I complimented her at length on what a successful re-creation it was of that wonderful moment. But she only chuckled and asked me if I had found the little joke she had made in the picture. Since I had come across nothing that would account for the degree of her private amusement, I searched further in the painting,

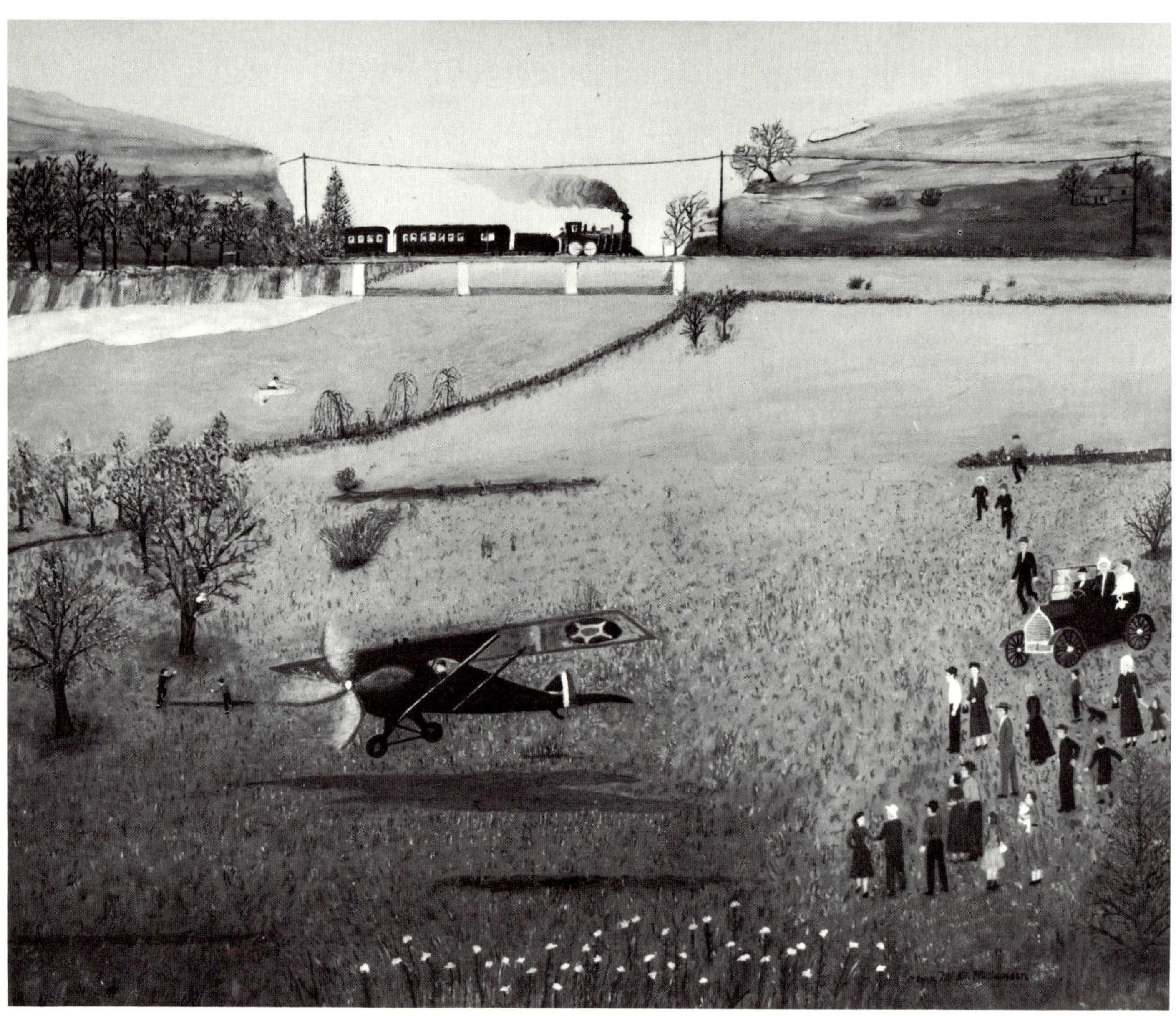

TRANSPORTATION, THE OLD AND THE NEW, CIRCA 1919, MERIDIAN, TEXAS
Oil on panel, 1963, 21 x 25¼ in.; courtesy Mr. and Mrs. Vincent A. Carrozza, Dallas

still finding nothing. She was delighted that her joke was so well hidden; she had painted the man in the rowboat rowing backwards instead of forwards. But she so often adds a touch of her unique humor to these memory paintings that it was unusual only that I could not spot it readily, and this gave her much pleasure.

Around 1920 Clara moved from Iredell, from this world she had known so intimately for over forty years. She had only the brief time in Waxahachie to give her a glimpse of what it was like to live elsewhere, of a world other than her small Texas country town. John's daughter, Faye, had married and moved to Dallas, and since he was particularly fond of his daughter and found himself missing her, John went off to the city to pay her a visit. He looked around a bit while there, liked what he saw, and returned home to discuss with Clara a move to Dallas. With little time wasted, he sold out everything that tied them to Iredell, and the Williamsons left for the city.

Clara was secretly pleased about the change although not the rapidity with which it was accomplished. It promised a release from the bondage she knew, and a wealth of new experiences and opportunities to be sought and enjoyed. For her Donald, who was still in high school, there were the obvious advantages of the city schools and their wealth of superior offerings over what could be found in Iredell. Further, John Williamson looked forward to using his many years of retailing experience in the service of some Dallas firm.

So the move was made with happy anticipation for all. They settled in the Oak Cliff section of Dallas, investing a portion of their new capital in a large house there. With native Scotch acumen, Clara promptly turned it into a rooming house, so there would be little loss of time in gaining an immediate and continuing return on their investment. This was work that she could handle with such ease, after her years of managing to hold down innumerable jobs at one and the same time, that it was almost like being in retirement.

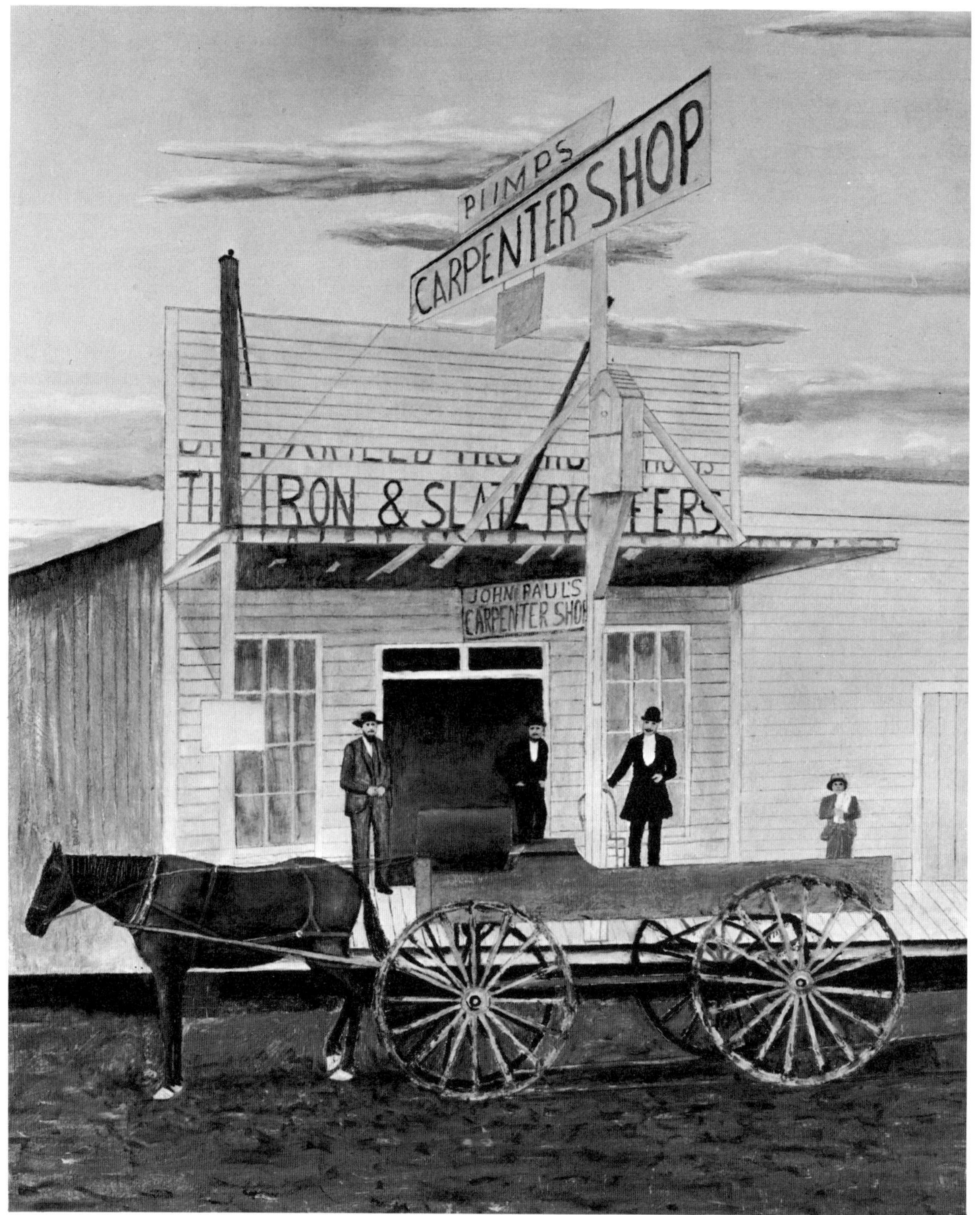

EARLY DALLAS
Oil on panel, 1951-1952, 24 x 20 in.; courtesy Mr. and Mrs. Albert Dorne, New York, New York

But as soon as she had settled comfortably into enjoyment of the seeming lightness of her load, John began to chafe at having nothing to do. So he inquired for employment at the wholesale houses where he was already acquainted and known from his many years as a customer, feeling that his experience would be thought invaluable. When he was refused he was very much upset and downhearted; it was indicated that he was too old and set in his ways — these businesses needed younger men who could be trained to suit the wholesalers' particular requirements.

He became more and more depressed, and worried constantly to Clara that they couldn't continue living as they were unless he found something to do that would bring in money. This finally wore down her resistance, and she reluctantly agreed that they go back into business. This, actually, was all John knew to do. So they traded some properties, built a new store, and, although it was a small business (as John put it, "Just something you and I can handle for ourselves, Clara"), the brief retirement was over and the hard work began again for Clara. In establishing this new business in the city, she found the work even harder than it had been in Iredell. She did nearly all the buying, but here it meant going to market and to the wholesale houses to select the goods, and for a different buying public than that she had had experience with. The worry was that if she didn't buy the right items they wouldn't sell, and if they couldn't be sold there was no profit to be made in spite of all the hard work. But as she became rich in city experience, as she had been in country know-how, this business, too, grew steadily and successfully.

Aunt Clara's painting *Early Dallas* records not the city as she saw and came to know it when she moved there to live, but a much earlier Dallas. It was inspired by a photograph taken possibly at about the time the Bosque River froze so hard, and by the stories her father had told her about Dallas when she was young. The carpenter shop in the photograph brought immediate memories of the time her father was called into the city by a machine company to set up a special exhibit on their behalf at the county fair, and his description of Dallas on his return to Iredell, which labeled it a town of black dirt and unpaved streets that became seas of black, sticky mud when it rained. And so she has painted *Early Dallas* in the somber shadings of the black-and-white photograph; and the mud her father described clings to the wheels of the wagon. But to make the painting unmistakably hers and to remove it totally from the photograph, she has devised the wagon in front of the store, and painted it an unbelievably beautiful shade of violet. With this extraordinary color, this haunting violet, she has claimed the painting for her own.

The Williamsons' store continued to do so well, as the years passed, that their location caught the eye of a gentleman who wished to own just such a business. He made them an excellent offer for the stock and good will they had built up (with the proviso, also, that he would rent the house and the store from them) and they accepted with little hesitation. John Williamson, no longer in the best of health, tired easily, and Clara was certainly eager to be free at last of the business; so they were both happy to sell out and to find themselves with leisure time.

Mr. Williamson promptly bought a car. As Aunt Clara put it, "He didn't even know how to drive — just went down and bought himself a car, and started right off driving. He could drive a horse all right, but that car, he couldn't drive it well. He was just so countrified, you wouldn't believe it. But it was just a Ford, a cheap little car, and he liked to drive it." And he drove everywhere and nearly all the time. Together they explored the Oak Cliff section from one end to the other, then crossed the Trinity River to the large area of Dallas, and started their daily tours there.

It wasn't until he was on his second car ("a fresh car," as she put it), that they one day decided to drive over and look around the University for the first time. There they found the property on which they built the home in which Aunt Clara lives today. They drove around the small campus and headed down Yale Boulevard — "There were just two houses on this street, one at either end, and the man who lived in one of these houses had a little dairy business — had milk cows, you know, and sold milk all around the area, and the cows were grazing down the street. And I said, 'I like that lot. It fronts to the south and would catch the breeze and I'd have such a pretty view.' And he said, 'Well, maybe we could buy it.' And I said, 'Well, I'd like to have it and have me a house right along here'."

So John hunted up the office and Clara picked out the exact lot she wanted, and they bought it right then — the highest lot on the street, "because I grew up on a hill, you know" — and built a home.

Clara loved it, for the area remained "country" for quite a long time, and she could walk out on her front porch and have a new picture to enjoy during each season of the year. "...it would change every autumn, spring, summer, and fall, and I'd work out there on my front plot and look at the fall colors and all. There were some little trees out there in groves, and grass, meadow grass, all around — and the birds flew over in flocks going south, or settled in the trees out there — and then, we could see the train come out of Dallas and go by this way. I painted it in that watercolor *Fast Train*. Time I painted that, I just looked out and saw it going by, and went in and painted the train and the valley as it was before everything changed here. You couldn't see that today, it's all so built up. Now you have to go outside and look straight up even to see the sky, that's the way it is!"

Although Clara was indeed pleased with her commodious new home (built sturdily of dark-red brick outside and pine paneling inside, and set as high as the land permitted) this was a most difficult period for her. John Williamson's health deteriorated at a slow but constant rate, and it wasn't long before he was even unable to drive. He stood this new restriction with its resultant immobility only so long; then one day when there was to be a parade in town that he particularly wanted to see he insisted that Clara take the wheel and drive him to the parade.

She had spent little time behind the wheel of a car; he had so enjoyed the act of driving, that she had no real desire to learn. And now, with scant preparation, she was being asked to just get in the car and drive him to town. She tried to beg off, feeling very unsure of her ability, but he overrode her objections, and before she quite knew what was happening, scared and shaking, she drove him right to the middle of the city, with one near mishap after another. As she said in telling me of this adventure, "I just don't know how we got there, and I know we like to never got home!" But from then on she drove the car with growing confidence, and took her increasingly infirm husband for daily drives, in attempts to give him a bit of pleasure and a respite from growing irritation and boredom.

In the evenings, after supper, as they sat before the fireplace and rocked a bit before retiring, she would occasionally work on a punch-work rug, holding it on her lap and enjoying the interplay of colors as she pushed the punch in and out. As she worked out each new facet of her design, John indicated quite strongly that such foolishness was a waste, and that Clara ought to spend her time instead on something that was worthwhile. She came to reply tartly that this was something worthwhile to her, and so the argument would continue as she continued to work on her rug. Even when the handsome rug was finished and proudly placed on the hearth, he continued to fuss about it, saying that it got in the way of his chair, and telling her to take it away. But in spite of this opposition, or because of it, there it remained, to be replaced by another as the first became worn. Clara made many of these intricately designed and colorful rugs, giving some away to relatives and storing some for herself. They were, as she calls it, her "artistic outlet." (There is still a punchwork rug in front of her fireplace — one with which I am now happily familiar, as it is a real beauty.)

It is unfortunate that John Williamson had not the temperament to take invalidism with any grace and that he was intermittently bed-ridden for over two years prior to his death in 1943. He preferred that Clara and only Clara do everything for him herself during these years, which, over such a lengthy period, proved exhausting for her. It was a very bad time for them both. Even now she cannot speak of it without obvious distaste and a shaking of her head as if by such a gesture she could dislodge memories that brought her no pleasure.

With Mr. Williamson's death, in the middle of that hot August, came release for them both. And at the age of sixty-eight, for the first time in her life, she says, "I was left alone, with nothing especially to do."

But Clara Williamson was not long in finding something *quite* special to do with this aloneness and new freedom. From earliest childhood, when she would lie on her back in a meadow under a tree and watch the sun patterns on the leaves and the changing cloud forms in the sky, she longed to communicate the beauty she found in all around her. And since this beauty was felt in form and color instead of in words, she had always wished she could sit quietly and sketch or draw what she had seen and felt — to share these experiences with others. Her moment for this had at last arrived, and she was quick to appreciate it.

She promptly started making sketches of everything around her — a chair, a table, a pretty vase, and she remembers in particular a profile she did of a handsome young woman who was rooming with her; for she also still took in roomers, and does to this day. She worked in pencil and charcoal; then bought and worked with watercolor, having somewhere picked up the erroneous idea that this medium was the simplest to use. She has often mentioned being glad that she started with watercolors; it made the oils seem so easy to control when she later made the change to them.

After experimenting briefly in this manner on her own, she enrolled as an auditor in a drawing class at Southern Methodist University in the fall of 1943. She didn't attend the class with any regularity; although a great believer in education, she sometimes found the subject at hand impertinent to her interests (for she already had in her head much of what she wanted to paint), and sometimes, quite simply, she found the flights of stairs that had to be climbed to reach the art class too much for her. But in or out of class she sketched and worked on her drawing as constantly as time would permit. Although she worked pretty much on her own in the classroom, she kept track of what the others were doing, and was fascinated one day by a lecture and demonstration on perspective "— and I just thought, well, that's so simple it's just pitiful. I didn't know the word, perspective — I didn't know what to call it — but I just knew I had to make a picture and use that in it."

During the following winter she found it more convenient to sit in on some of the evening painting classes at the Dallas Museum School than to return to SMU, and she continued in pleasant, though sporadic attendance there through the winter of 1946. She enjoyed the Museum class; in part because she had friends who were studying there who could give her companionship as well as transportation; but also because the class involved a most varied age group and was composed of grown men and women, all with different backgrounds, talent, and intent. She was more comfortable in such a group than she had been with the very young University students, who were all beginners in life as well as in art. And the man who presided over these students at the Museum was both kind and wise, and had the special wisdom to encourage Aunt Clara in her painting with the least possible interference and guidance.

In this relaxed and congenial atmosphere, Aunt Clara began and completed her first memory picture, *Chicken for Dinner,* and it was while she was working on this, sitting off to the side of the classroom all by herself, that I first had the pleasure of meeting her, as I have described in the beginning of this account. Before this she had painted from still life set-ups, occasionally from a live model in the classroom, and at home had painted everything and everyone she found around her. But now she was at last ready to put on canvas the many scenes and thoughts she had carried in her mind for almost seventy years. It was an exciting time.

By the spring of 1945 she was already not only entering the local competitive exhibitions, but winning purchase prizes and other awards in them, much to the surprise of a good portion of the rest of the artistic community, and at first, to Aunt Clara, herself. Many disgruntled artists could not understand her success, and found her ingenuous vision crude; but another group of painters, of whom I was one, found her painting exciting and a completely valid artistic expression. Aunt Clara was greatly encouraged by the obvious admiration of the artists who found worth in her paintings, and she was always modestly bemused by their praise, as she was quite in awe of some of them. But she did enjoy being with these new friends, and she became an aware and interested fixture at the Museum exhibition openings, finding stimulation from talking with persons for whom art was a way of life, and from being in such a dedicated amosphere. This was a new and fascinating world and one in which perhaps she did not by nature and background belong; but for her, each foray into it brought a bit of glamor and high adventure. This had little relation to the world that was hers in Iredell, or even in Waxahachie, or in Dallas during the early years.

Honors continued to come Aunt Clara's way in the world of art, but she was unaffected by them except that they induced her to continue painting, in her own manner, "the good, the true, and the beautiful," and to concentrate more of her time on it. To the artists and others who came to know her personally, she was sanity and fresh air, with a canniness and charm and humor that made each long to count her among his dearest relatives. Perhaps this is why it was so natural for so many to adopt her as "Aunt Clara," once the name had been given.

The conferral of this name occurred in 1951 at a club in Dallas where Betty McLean was giving an elegant dinner party to honor the nine Texas artists whom she had selected to form the nucleus of her new gallery. Mrs. Williamson, who was practically the first of the nine to be invited, was seated at the foot of the long table next to Mr. McLean. She leaned toward him to begin a conversation, saying,

"Mr. McLean —" but she got no farther, as he promptly said,

"Please don't call me, 'Mr. McLean' . . . call me 'Jock'." She countered with

"Well, I'll call you 'Jock,' if you call me 'Clara'." His response being,

"I couldn't quite do that, so I'll call you 'Aunt Clara.' How will that be?"

It must have been quite acceptable, as the name "Aunt Clara" was promptly passed around the table and taken up by all present. It proved to be so appropriate that it has been used ever since by all who become acquainted with Clara Williamson through love of her paintings.

And those paintings have been many and marvelously varied through the years, for in addition to the memory pictures, on which we have more or less concentrated here, there are also the many pictures that have to do with contemporary happenings, and those of a religious or purely imaginative nature.

Some of the subjects that impressed her and that she recorded from the contemporary scene are *The Baptism, The Rodeo, Dallas Post Office, Dallas Symphony Orchestra* (with all ninety-eight members, plus conductor and soloist), *Basket of Lilacs,* varied scenes around the University grounds next door, and a most interesting and humorous painting of *The Art Gallery,* in which she has attempted to reproduce on the gallery walls an example of every type and style of painting she can conceive, and the audience for each.

She traveled little, but the two trips that she made to visit her son Donald brought also their permanent rewards in paint. When he lived in Louisiana she made her first airplane flight to Baton Rouge (". . . it felt just as it had in my dream — flying, that is — just exactly . . .") and on her return painted a delicate and meticulous watercolor of an *Old French Court,* and an oil, *Baton Rouge Bridge* as seen from the airplane. She spent one Christmas in New York City with Donald, and on being shown the sights of New York was most impressed with the Christmas decorations and the skaters at Rockefeller Plaza. So this trip produced the enchanting *Radio City Christmas Tree, 1949,* with its delightful skaters performing their graceful rituals. There are, of course, many more.

The same is true with the pictures she has done that deal with religious subjects or with dreams and imaginings. For there are *The Glory Train, My House Has Many Mansions,* and *The Ten Commandments;* though that names only a few that deal with religion while verging on fantasy — and in the purely imaginative vein, among others, there are *The Veteran's Dream* and two lovely ones concerning nature: *Where Man Does Not Molest* (a scene endowed with natural abundance) and *Spring, Above and Below.*

Aunt Clara has created in *Spring, Above and Below,* a landscape that is the epitome of springtime, with pristine new leaves and blossoms covering the branches of the trees; the first wild flowers blooming daintily by a placid pond; the birds and animals nesting and burrowing and pairing off in spring fervor. To show more fully the wonder of nature, and to emphasize that spring occurs beneath the earth and water as it does on the surface — that *all* is spring — she has sliced across the lower earth and water to paint the fingering roots of the trees and bushes branching out in the dirt, and the more delicate rootlets of the grass and smaller plants. She leads us beneath the surface of the pond to peek with a duck that has dipped his head through the water line, and to enjoy, under the water, the fish, as they frolic with their young. The coloring in this painting is the tenderest spring green, and pink and white; with accents from the flashing red of cardinals and the blue of jays, all underlaid with the rich brown of the earth beneath. She presents us with the miracle of growth and the renewal of spring, and we feel it occurring in her painting. A bit of magic seems always present in her work.

Aunt Clara prepared a serious and studied statement of her aims and intentions for an exhibition catalogue in 1952, that went as follows:

"There is nothing unusual or especially interesting in my efforts in the art of painting. I try to paint because of the love of the art.

"I am an elderly widow, and, perhaps because of a sense of appro-

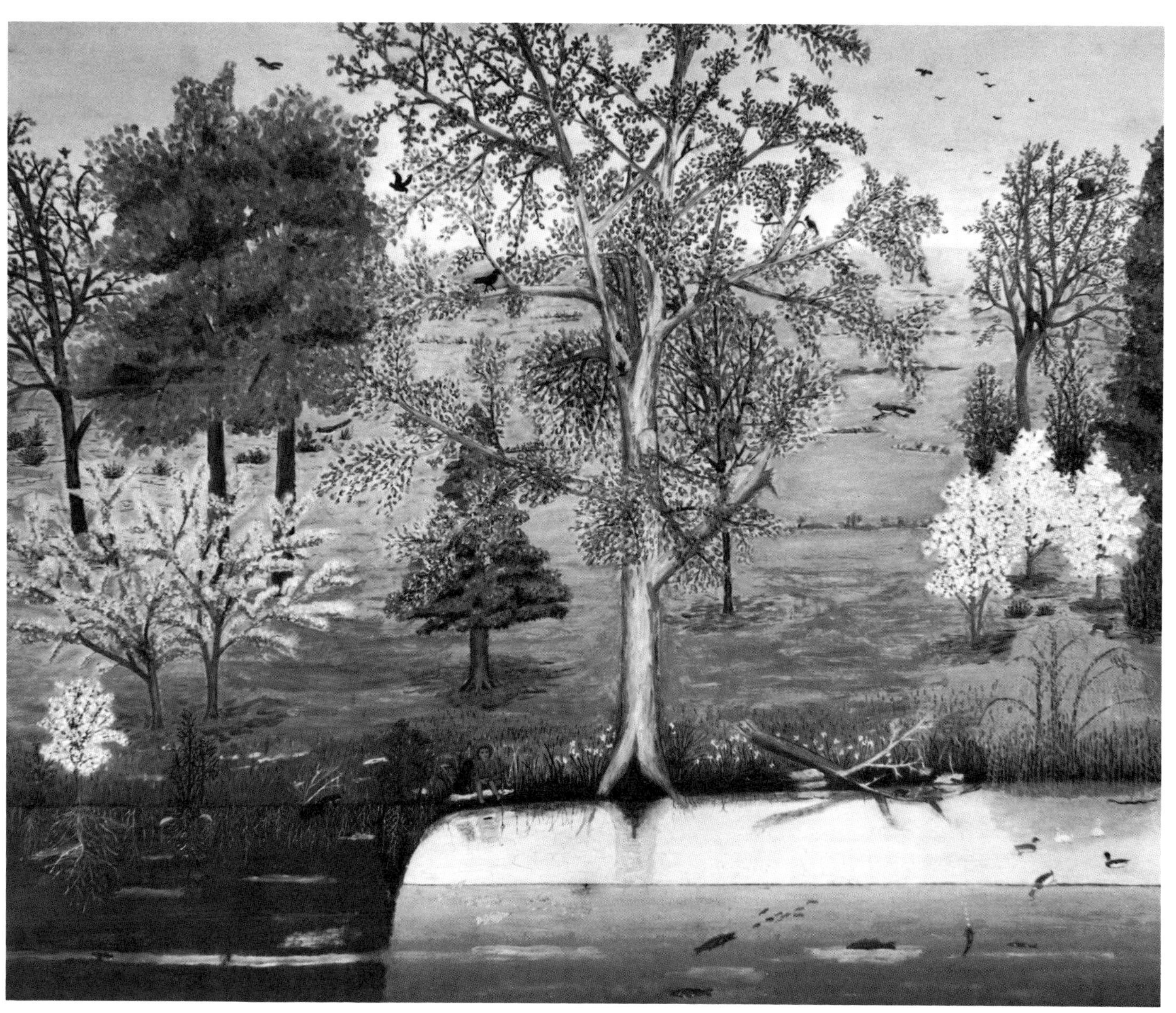

SPRING ABOVE AND BELOW
Oil on panel, 1948-1949, 24 x 30 in.; courtesy Mr. and Mrs. H. Ben Decherd, Jr., Dallas

priateness to my age and experience, I try to accomplish realism, truth, beauty, and some amusement in my pictures. . . .

"I often try to record my memories in my paintings, and I feel sure that I succeed, at least in the truthfulness of the subject though not in any degree of perfection of execution. I have never yet made a painting that measured up to my mental picture of the subject; yet it is always a challenge to try."

To paraphrase this for my own account: I feel sure that I succeed at least in the truthfulness of the subject, though not in any degree of perfection of execution in writing "Aunt Clara." And if I have not transmitted an image that measures up to my mental picture of Clara McDonald Williamson the attempt to do so has indeed been an exciting challenge.

APPENDIXES

APPENDIX A. EXHIBITIONS IN WHICH PAINTINGS BY CLARA WILLIAMSON WERE SHOWN
(Including Awards Won by Her Work)

1945 Sixteenth Annual Dallas Allied Arts Exhibit
Dallas Museum of Fine Arts, Dallas
Raiberto Comini Purchase Award

1946 Seventeenth Annual Dallas Allied Arts Exhibit
Dallas Museum of Fine Arts, Dallas
Dealey Purchase Award

1946 Pepsi-Cola "Painting of the Year" Invitational Exhibition
National Academy of Design, New York, New York

1946 Two Hundred Years of American Painting
Dallas Museum of Fine Arts, Dallas

1946 The Eighth Texas General Exhibition
Dallas Museum of Fine Arts, Dallas
Museum of Fine Arts, Houston
Witte Memorial Museum, San Antonio

1947 Eighteenth Annual Dallas Allied Arts Exhibit
Dallas Museum of Fine Arts, Dallas
Mr. and Mrs. Raiberto Comini Award

1948 One-Man Show
Dallas Museum of Fine Arts, Dallas

1948 Nineteenth Annual Dallas Allied Arts Exhibit
Dallas Museum of Fine Arts, Dallas

1948 One-Man Show
Elisabet Ney Museum, Austin

1949 Twentieth Annual Dallas Allied Arts Exhibit
Dallas Museum of Fine Arts, Dallas

1950 American Painting of Today, 1950
Metropolitan Museum of Art, New York, New York

1950 Twenty-First Annual Dallas Allied Arts Exhibit
Dallas Museum of Fine Arts, Dallas
Anonymous Cash Award

1951 Texas Wildcat Show,
Fort Worth Art Association, Fort Worth

1951 Thirteenth Annual Texas Painting and Sculpture Exhibition
Witte Memorial Museum, San Antonio
Museum of Fine Arts, Houston
Dallas Museum of Fine Arts, Dallas
Honorable Mention Award

1952 Texas Watercolor Society Exhibition
San Antonio
Silver Platter Award

1952 Terry National Art Exhibition
Terry Art Institute, Miami, Florida
Sixth Purchase Prize

1952 Texas Fine Arts Association Membership Exhibition
Austin

1952 Texas Contemporary Artists
M. Knoedler & Company, Inc., New York, New York

1952 Fourteenth Annual Exhibition of Texas Painting and Sculpture
Dallas Museum of Fine Arts, Dallas
Museum of Fine Arts, Houston
Witte Memorial Museum, San Antonio
Humble Oil & Refining Company Award

1953 University of Illinois Exhibition of
Contemporary Paintings and Sculpture
University of Illinois, Urbana, Illinois

1953 One-Man Show
Betty McLean Gallery, Dallas

1953 Fourteenth Annual Artists West of the Mississippi Invitational
Colorado Springs Fine Arts Center, Colorado Springs, Colorado

1953 Group Exhibition: Artists from Betty McLean Gallery
Santa Barbara Museum of Art, Santa Barbara, California
Frank Perls Gallery, Beverly Hills, California

1953 State Fair of Texas Exhibition (Fifteenth Texas Annual)
Dallas Museum of Fine Arts, Dallas
Museum of Fine Arts, Houston
Witte Memorial Museum, San Antonio

1953-1954 American Contemporary Natural Painters
Invitational traveling exhibition sponsored by the
Smithsonian Institution, Washington, D.C.

1954 Twenty-Fifth Annual Dallas Allied Arts Exhibit
Dallas Museum of Fine Arts, Dallas
Summerfield G. Roberts Award

1954 One-Man Show
The Alan Gallery, New York, New York

1954 Man and His Years Exhibition
Baltimore Museum of Art, Baltimore, Maryland

1954-1955 American Primitive Paintings
Assembled by the Smithsonian Institution for travel
in Europe and Scandinavia

1954-1955 American Natural Painters
Invitational traveling exhibition sponsored by the
Smithsonian Institution, Washington, D.C.

1955 Altrusa Club of Dallas
Mature Woman's Award
(An award presented annually to a woman who began a
successful career after the age of forty)

1955 Pittsburgh International Invitation Exhibition
Carnegie Institute, Pittsburgh, Pennsylvania

1955 Seventeenth Annual Texas General Exhibition
Dallas Museum of Fine Arts, Dallas
Witte Memorial Museum, San Antonio
Texas Fine Arts Association, Austin
Fort Worth Art Center, Fort Worth

1956 Twenty-Seventh Annual Dallas Allied Arts Exhibit
Dallas Museum of Fine Arts, Dallas
Neiman-Marcus Award

1956 One-Man Show
First National Bank Building, San Antonio

1956 Executive View, Art in the Office
Assembled by the American Federation of Arts
Exhibited at the Time-Life Building, New York, New York

1956 Eighteenth Annual Texas Exhibition of Painting and Sculpture
Dallas Museum of Fine Arts, Dallas
Texas Fine Arts, Austin
The Museum, Lubbock
Museum of Fine Arts, Houston
Witte Memorial Museum, San Antonio

1957 D. D. Feldman Exhibition of Texas Art
Dallas

1957 A Survey of Texas Painting
Dallas Museum of Fine Arts, Dallas

1957 University of Illinois Biennial Invitation Exhibition
University of Illinois, Urbana, Illinois

1957 State Fair of Texas Exhibition (Nineteenth Texas General)
Dallas Museum of Fine Arts, Dallas
Museum of Fine Arts, Houston
Witte Memorial Museum, San Antonio
Beaumont Museum, Beaumont

1958 Exhibition of Naive Painters
Madison Square Garden antique show
Galerie St. Etienne, New York, New York

1958 Natural Painters Exhibition
Southampton, New York

1958 Religious Arts of the Western World
Dallas Museum of Fine Arts, Dallas

1958 The Iron Horse in Art
Fort Worth Art Center, Fort Worth

1958 Texas Oil, 1958
Dallas Public Library, Dallas

1958 D. D. Feldman Exhibition of Texas Painting
Dallas Public Library, Dallas

1958-1959 American Primitive Painting Exhibition
Invitational traveling exhibition sponsored by the
Smithsonian Institution, Washington, D.C.

1959 One-Man Show
First National Bank, Dallas

1959 Made in Texas by Texans
Dallas Museum for Contemporary Arts, Dallas

1959 State Fair of Texas Exhibition (Twenty-First Texas General)
Dallas Museum of Fine Arts, Dallas
Museum of Fine Arts, Houston
Witte Memorial Museum, San Antonio

1960 Southwestern Art: Painters of Arizona, Arkansas,
Colorado, Louisiana, New Mexico, Oklahoma, and Texas
Dallas Museum of Fine Arts, Dallas

1961 Young Collections Exhibition
Philbrook Museum, Tulsa, Oklahoma

1961 Ex-Students Exhibition
Southern Methodist University, Dallas

1961 A Century of Art and Life in Texas
Dallas Museum of Fine Arts, Dallas

1961 Paintings by Grandma Moses, Clara Williamson and H. O. Kelly
Fort Worth Art Center, Fort Worth

1962 One-Man Show
Fifth Avenue Gallery, Fort Worth

1962 One-Man Show
Stewart-Rickard Gallery, San Antonio

1962 One-Man Show
Junior Service League of Longview, Longview

1963 American Primitive Paintings Today
Bianchini Gallery, New York, New York

1964 One-Man Show
Valley House Gallery, Dallas

1966 The American Woman as Artist, 1820-1965
Pollock Galleries, Owen Fine Arts Center,
Southern Methodist University, Dallas

1966 International Naive Art
La Boetie, Inc., New York, New York

1966 International Exhibition of Primitive Art
Bratislava, Czechoslovakia

APPENDIX B. CHRONOLOGICAL LIST OF CLARA WILLIAMSON PAINTINGS

This chronological list of paintings is as nearly complete as concentrated research
and years of recordkeeping could make it. The blank spaces in some entries indicate that,
at the time of printing, the information needed was not available.—The Authors.

1943 Autumn Leaves
Oil on panel, 20 x 7 in.
Valley House Gallery, Dallas

1943 Cactus Blooms
Oil on panel, 20 x 7 in.
Valley House, Gallery, Dallas

1944 Bluebonnets
Oil on panel, 5 x 8 in.
Mrs. Alta Bradley, Dallas

1944 Fair Park Scene
Oil on canvas, 18½ x 12 in.
Mrs. W. A. Balendonck, Fullerton, California

1944 Radio & TV Tower in Fair Park (WRR)
Watercolor, 24 x 16 in.
Mr. and Mrs. Alton Appleby, Dallas

1944 Scene on the Deer Range, South Texas
Oil on panel, 21½ x 15½ in.
Mr. and Mrs. Alton Appleby, Dallas

1944 Still Life with Peppers †
Oil on canvas, 24 x 18 in.
Valley House Gallery, Dallas

1944 The Veteran's Dream †
Oil on panel, 24 x 30 in.
Valley House Gallery, Dallas

1944-1945 Disagreement
Oil on panel, 9 x 12 in.
Mr. Harry Brodnax, Dallas

1945 The Baptism (Baptizing) †
Oil on panel, 21½ x 19½ in.
Mr. and Mrs. William W. Wigley, Dallas

1945 Chicken for Dinner*†
Oil on canvas, 22½ x 30¼ in.
Mr. and Mrs. Donald S. Vogel, Dallas

1945 Copy of Mother's Painting
Oil

1945 Country House
Watercolor

1945 Get Along Little Dogies (Git 'Long Little Dogies) *†
Oil on canvas, 26¾ x 39¾ in.
Dallas Museum of Fine Arts, Dallas

1945 Breaking the Bronco †
Oil on canvas, 35 x 22¼ in.
Valley House Gallery, Dallas

1945 Dallas Skyline Looking South †
Oil on canvas, 17½ x 23½ in.
Dallas Museum of Fine Arts, Dallas

1945 Fast Train †
Watercolor, 22 x 29 in.
Mr. and Mrs. Jerry Bywaters, Dallas

1945-1946 The Girls Went Fishing*†
Oil on canvas, 24 x 36½ in.
Mr. John R. McLean, West Palm Beach, Florida

1946 A Day's Work Is Done*†
Oil on panel, 28 x 39¾ in.
Amon Carter Museum, Fort Worth

1946 Art Class, SMU
Oil on panel

1946 Bridge, Iredell †
Watercolor, 18½ x 30½ in.
Mr. Charles W. Mulcahy, Boston, Massachusetts

1946 Carding the Batts
Oil on panel, 11½ x 13 in.
Frances J. Greenwell, Dallas

1946 The Cowboy
Oil

1946 Early Christmas
Oil on panel, 11½ x 13 in.
Frances J. Greenwell, Dallas

1946 In Search of Black Gold (Oil)
Oil on panel
Mr. John R. McLean, West Palm Beach, Florida

*Pictures reproduced herein
†Pictures included in the exhibition

1946 The Lovers
Oil on Panel, 5½ x 9 in.
Mr. and Mrs. W. T. Rea, Dallas

1946 Man Plowing*†
Charcoal, 23 x 29 in.
Mrs. Tom Beckett, Jr., New Hope

1946 The Oaks
Watercolor, 22¼ x 30 in.
Valley House Gallery, Dallas

1946 Sunset on the Duffau
Pastel, 27¾ x 15 in.
Mrs. W. A. Balendonck, Fullerton, California

1946-1947 The Bridge, Iredell
Oil on panel, 17½ x 29½ in.
Mr. and Mrs. Vincent A. Carrozza, Dallas

1946-1947 Buggy on the Bridge
Oil on panel, 15½ x 7½ in.
Mr. and Mrs. Wes Wise, Dallas

1946-1947 Drought Ration*†
Oil on Panel, 20 x 24⅛ in.
Washington Art Galleries, Miami Beach, Florida

1946-1947 Fruit and Stool
Oil

1946-1947 Paluxy Creek: Tranquility*†
Watercolor, 17 x 23 in.
Mr. and Mrs. A. C. Swygard, Dallas

1946-1947 To the Eighteenth Hole
Oil

1947 Azaleas, Turtle Creek
Watercolor, 20 x 30 in.
Valley House Gallery, Dallas

1947 Bridge over the Mississippi
Oil on panel, 28 x 40 in.
Valley House Gallery, Dallas

1947 Dallas Symphony Orchestra †
Oil on panel, 17¼ x 36⅜ in.
Valley House Gallery, Dallas

1947 Evening Star
Oil on panel, 20 x 24 in.
Valley House Gallery, Dallas

1947 The Jitterbugs
Oil

1947 Mirror Reflections †
Oil on panel, 24 x 18 in.
Valley House Gallery, Dallas

1947 Mother Love on the Range
Oil on panel, 13 x 12 in.
Mrs. R. G. Williams, Houston

1947 Oil Derrick †
Oil on panel, 24 x 30 in.
Valley House Gallery, Dallas

1947 Old French Court †
Watercolor, 22¾ x 15½ in.
Mr. and Mrs Abe Ravkind, Dallas

1947 Standing in the Need of Prayer*†
Oil on panel, 28 x 40 in.
Mr. and Mrs. Dan C. Williams, Dallas

1947 Teeing Off
Oil on panel, 18 x 24 in.
Mr. and Mrs. A. R. Frank, Grapevine

1948 Catching up with Santa
Oil on panel, 10 x 16 in.
Mr. and Mrs. Wes Wise, Dallas

1948 Child Chased by Steer Series (four paintings)
Oil on panel, 8 x 10 in. each

1948 Georgie †
Oil on panel, 19½ x 17 in.
Valley House Gallery, Dallas

1948 Mountaineer's Dream
Oil on panel, 24 x 18 in.
Valley House Gallery, Dallas

1948 My Bow in the Cloud †
Oil on panel, 22 x 28 in.
Valley House Gallery, Dallas

*Pictures reproduced herein
†Pictures included in the exhibition

1948 Pet Cow Series (four paintings) †
Oil on panel, 9¼ x 13 in. each
Frances J. Greenwell, Dallas

1948 Rodeo †
Watercolor, 22½ x 29½ in.
Mrs. G. Richard Davis, New York, New York

1948 Self-Portrait
Oil on panel, 24 x 29¾ in.
Valley House Gallery, Dallas

1948 Self-Portrait
Oil on panel, 19 x 17 in.
Valley House Gallery, Dallas

1948-1949 Spring Above and Below*†
Oil on panel, 24 x 30 in.
Mr. and Mrs. H. Ben Decherd, Jr., Dallas

1949 The Art Gallery: Variety of Opinions †
Oil on panel, 18 x 42 in.
Valley House Gallery, Dallas

1949 Equestrian Lovers
Oil on panel, 12 x 10½ in.
Mr. and Mrs. Charles E. Schillinger, El Paso

1949 Riders on the River Trail
Oil on panel, 9 x 12 in.
Miss Bess Morgan, Dallas

1949 The Schillinger Family
Oil on canvas, 36 x 20 in.
Mr. and Mrs. Charles E. Schillinger, El Paso

1949 White Sands, New Mexico: Moonlight †
Oil on panel, 24 x 30 in.
Valley House Gallery, Dallas

1949 White Sands, New Mexico: Sunset
Oil on panel, 24 x 30 in.
Valley House Gallery, Dallas

1949-1950 The Building of the Railroad*†
Oil on panel, 27 x 29½ in.
Mr. and Mrs. Edward Douglas Cobb, Dallas

1949-1950 Radio City Christmas Tree, 1949†
Oil on panel, 24½ x 28 in.
Mr. and Mrs. Julius Cohen, New York, New York

1950 Bridge on Turtle Creek †
Watercolor, 12 x 17¾ in.
Valley House Gallery, Dallas

1950 Self-Portrait †
Oil on panel, 19½ x 17 in.
Valley House Gallery, Dallas

1950-1951 Main Street, Iredell*†
Oil on panel, 20 x 24 in.
Mr. and Mrs. Howell Smith, Dallas

1951 The Dream*†
Oil on panel, 25 x 21 in.
Mrs. Elizabeth Kennard, San Marcos

1951 Texas Barn Dance*†
Oil on panel, 24 x 36 in.
Dr. and Mrs. Malcolm B. Bowers, Dallas

1951-1952 Autumn Outing*†
Oil on panel, 48 x 60 in.
Mr. and Mrs. Waldo Stewart, Dallas

1951-1952 Early Dallas*
Oil on panel, 24 x 20 in.
Mr. and Mrs. Albert Dorne, New York, New York

1952 Bulldogging †
Oil on panel, 8½ x 11½ in.
Mrs. Robert D. Stecker, Dallas

1952 Landscape with Running Horses
Oil on panel, 8 x 26½ in.
Valley House Gallery, Dallas

1952 Mountain Road
Oil on panel, 24 x 23¼ in.
Miss Martha McCluney, Dallas

1952 Old Chisholm Trail*†
Oil on panel, 24 x 36½ in.
Wichita Art Museum, Roland P. Murdock Collection, Wichita, Kansas

*Pictures reproduced herein
†Pictures included in the exhibition

1952-1953 Cottonpickers t
Oil on panel, 7½ x 9½ in.
Mrs. Robert D. Stecker, Dallas

1952-1953 Cotton-Picking Time*t
Oil on panel, 24 x 27 in.
Texas Bank & Trust Company, Dallas

1952-1953 Dallas Post Office t
Oil on panel, 28 x 26 in.
Dr. and Mrs. Buck J. Wynne. Jr., Dallas

1952-1953 For Keeps t
Oil on canvas, 18 x 24 in.
Mrs. Violet Hayden Dowell, Dallas

1953 Aunt Fanny's Garden t
Oil on panel, 11 x 13 in.
Mr. and Mrs. Jerome K. Crossman, Dallas

1953 Basket of Lilacs t
Oil on panel, 18½ x 22 in.
Valley House Gallery, Dallas

1953 The Day the Bosque Froze Over or Winter on the Bosque*
Oil on panel, 20 x 28 in.
Collection, The Museum of Modern Art, New York, New York
Gift of Albert Dorne

1953 Harvest Hands at Dinner*t
Oil on panel, 24 x 40 in.
Mrs. Amelia Anderson Fuller, Dallas

1953 High Spirits t
Oil on panel, 11 x 14 in.
Mr. and Mrs. Henry W. Frost, Jr., Dallas

1953 Picnic for Two
Oil on canvas, 16¼ x 13½ in.
Mr. and Mrs. James Lovell, Dallas

1953 Pipe Truck
Oil on panel, 8 x 10⅞ in.
Valley House Gallery, Dallas

1953 The Quilting Bee t
Oil on canvas, 24 x 26 in.
Mr. Bill M. Womack, Dallas

1953 Sunday Train*t
Oil on panel, 24 x 32 in.
Mr. Robert T. Vanderbilt, Gstaad, Switzerland

1953 Three on a Horse t
Oil on panel, 9¾ x 12¾ in.
Mr. Otto Kallir, New York, New York

1953 Traveling by Rail t
Oil on panel, 18 x 20 in.
Valley House Gallery, Dallas

1953 Virginia Reel t
Oil on panel, 15 x 18 in.
Mr. and Mrs. Julius Cohen, New York, New York

1953-1954 Mother's Work Basket t
Oil on panel, 20 x 24 in.
Valley House Gallery, Dallas

1954 Dinner at May's Boarding House t
Oil on panel, 16 x 24 in.
Valley House Gallery, Dallas

1954 Fishing on the Duffau*t
Oil on panel, 18 x 30 in.
Mr. and Mrs. Denys R. Slater, Jr., Dallas

1954 The Visitor t
Oil on canvas, 19 x 19 in.
Mr. and Mrs. William D. Kyle, Jr., Milwaukee, Wisconsin

1954 The Harvest*t
Oil on panel, 20½ x 28¼ in.
The Stewart Company, Dallas

1954 The Night before Christmas*t
Oil on panel, 18 x 24 in.
Miss Suzanne Simmons, Dallas

1954 The Produce Man's Visit*t
Oil on panel, 15½ x 19½ in.
Mrs. Elizabeth Kennard, San Marcos

1954 Unwilling Churner t
Oil on panel, 9 x 12 in.
Mr. and Mrs. James F. Chambers, Jr., Dallas

*Pictures reproduced herein
tPictures included in the exhibition

1954-1955 Laying the Pipeline
Oil on panel

1955 The Blacksmith Shop*†
Oil on panel, 18 x 30 in.
Dr. and Mrs. P. M. Williamson, Dayton, Ohio

1955 The Circuit Rider*†
Oil on panel, 21 x 25 in.
Mr. and Mrs. H. Ben Decherd, Jr., Dallas

1955 The Family Room*†
Oil on panel, 15 x 22½ in.
Dr. and Mrs. P. M. Williamson, Dayton, Ohio

1955 Heavy Traffic on a Country Road †
Oil on panel, 15 x 22½ in.
Dr. and Mrs. Malcolm B. Bowers, Dallas

1955 Monday*†
Oil on panel, 18 x 24 in.
Mr. and Mrs. John W. O'Boyle, Dallas

1955 Offshore Fishing †
Oil on canvas, 16 x 24 in.
Mr. and Mrs. O. D. Buford, Dallas

1955 Siamese Kitten
Oil on panel, 8 x 10 in.
Mr. and Mrs. James F. Chambers, Jr., Dallas

1955 Square Dance*
Oil on panel, 15 x 25 in.
Valley House Gallery, Dallas

1955 Sweet Adeline*†
Oil on panel, 18 x 24 in.
Mr. and Mrs. Thomas N. Overton, Dallas

1955 View of Dallas †
Oil on panel, 22 x 36 in.
Valley House Gallery, Dallas

1955-1956 The Night Hunters*†
Oil on panel, 24 x 27 in.
Mr. Robert W. Decherd, Dallas

1955-1956 Pappy Crone's Cabin*†
Oil on panel, 18 x 24 in.
Mr. and Mrs. A. R. Frank, Grapevine

1956 Paluxy Creek*
Oil on panel, 22 x 33½ in.
Miss Ann A. Lafferty, Dallas

1957 Arbor Meeting*†
Oil on panel, 30 x 48 in.
Dr. and Mrs. Malcolm B. Bowers, Dallas

1957 Chore Time †
Oil on panel, 16 x 20 in.
Mrs. Burton Gilliland, Dallas

1957 Country Club
Oil on panel, 9 x 12 in.
Valley House Gallery, Dallas

1957 Foursome
Oil on panel, 10 x 12 in.
Mrs. Jack Munger, Dallas

1957 Golfer
Oil on panel, 7 x 10 in.
Valley House Gallery, Dallas

1957 Playground †
Oil on panel, 8 x 12 in.
Mrs. Foster Yancey, Dallas

1957 Roping on the Range †
Oil on panel, 18 x 20 in.
Dr. M. C. Overton III, Galveston

1957 Sand Trap
Oil on panel, 7 x 9 in.
Mr. Wilson Schoellkopf, Jr., Dallas

1957 The Ten Commandments
Oil on panel, 22 x 30 in.
Valley House Gallery, Dallas

1957-1958 The Grist Mill
Oil on panel, 18 x 22 in.
The Right Reverend and Mrs. Joseph M. Harte, Phoenix, Arizona

*Pictures reproduced herein
†Pictures included in the exhibition

1957-1958 Landscape by Moonlight
Oil on canvas, 24 x 18 in.
Valley House Gallery, Dallas

1957-1958 The Swollen Creek †
Oil on panel, 20 x 24 in.
Dr. and Mrs. William T. Bowers, Dallas

1958 Backyard Dispute †
Oil on panel, 9 x 12 in.
Valley House Gallery, Dallas

1958 Bringing Home the Christmas Tree †
Oil on canvas, 17½ x 23½ in.
Dr. and Mrs. F. L. Whittlesey, Dallas

1958 Getting Ready for Santa †
Oil on panel, 22 x 27½ in.
Valley House Gallery, Dallas

1958 Easter
Oil on panel, 18 x 24 in.
Valley House Gallery, Dallas

1958 The Rabbit Hunt
Oil on panel, 10 x 20 in.
Mr. and Mrs. Wes Wise, Dallas

1958 Rider on a White Horse
Oil, 8 x 16 in.

1958 Young Painter in Landscape
Oil, 12 x 18 in.

1959 The Little Country Church
Oil on panel, 18 x 21 in.
Mr. Ralph P. Jones, Dallas

1959 Little Town Train
Oil on panel, 18 x 21 in.
Mr. Ralph P. Jones, Dallas

1959 Village on the Bosque, 1890*†
Oil on panel, 38 x 48 in.
Mr. and Mrs. John L. Paxton, Fort Worth

1959 Where Man Does Not Molest †
Oil on panel, 30 x 36 in.
Miss Ann A. Lafferty, Dallas

1960 Before the Rainstorm
Oil on panel, 24 x 28 in.
Valley House Gallery, Dallas

1960 The Old Homeplace †
Oil on canvas, 14 x 18 in.
Mr. and Mrs. Jay R. Huckabee, Snyder

1960 Caretaker †
Oil on panel, 8 x 10 in.
Mr. and Mrs. Wirt Davis II, Dallas

1960 The Glory Train †
Oil on panel, 22 x 29 in.
Miss Dealey Decherd, Dallas

1960 Golf Cart
Oil on panel, 14 x 20 in.
Valley House Gallery, Dallas

1960 A Modern Lady
Oil on panel, 15⅞ x 12 in.
Valley House Gallery, Dallas

1960 Mother Love
Oil on panel, 12 x 16 in.
Mr. and Mrs. Thomas Massey, Dallas

1960 Preparing the Batts †
Oil on panel, 18 x 20¾ in.
Valley House Gallery, Dallas

1960-1961 At the Old Swimming Hole*†
Oil on panel, 24 x 38 in.
Valley House Gallery, Dallas

1960-1961 The Gordon Schoolhouse*†
Oil on panel, 30 x 40 in.
Valley House Gallery, Dallas

1961 The Garden of Prayer †
Oil on panel, 30 x 40 in.
Valley House Gallery, Dallas

1961 On Our Way †
Oil on panel, 25 x 28 in.
Mr. Joseph P. Donahue, Jr., Lowell, Massachusetts

*Pictures reproduced herein
†Pictures included in the exhibition

1961 Riders in the Snow
Oil on panel, 24 x 18 in.
Valley House Gallery, Dallas

1962 First Automobile Ride*†
Oil on canvas, 20 x 30 in.
Dr. and Mrs. Earl L. Carter, Dallas

1963 Transportation, the Old and the New, circa 1919, Meridian, Texas*†
Oil on panel, 21 x 25¼ in.
Mr. and Mrs. Vincent A. Carrozza, Dallas

1964 Chandor Garden, Weatherford †
Oil on panel, 36 x 24 in.
Valley House Gallery, Dallas

1964 Streetcar, Waxahachie*†
Oil on panel, 15 x 24 in.
Valley House Gallery, Dallas

1965 Frontier Carpenter Shop*†
Oil on canvas, 26 x 30 in.
Valley House Gallery, Dallas

1966 Early Texas Cowboy †
Oil on panel, 12 x 17 in.
Valley House Gallery, Dallas

1966 Fishermen at Duffau Falls †
Oil on panel, 18¼ x 26¼ in.
Valley House Gallery, Dallas

1966 Free Watermelon Party †
Oil on panel, 17½ x 27 in.
Mr. and Mrs. Dan C. Williams, Dallas

1966 My Birthplace*†
Oil on canvas, 24 x 30 in.
Dr. and Mrs. P. M. Williamson, Dayton, Ohio

*Pictures reproduced herein
†Pictures included in the exhibition

BOOK DESIGN AND PRODUCTION: CRAWFORD DUNN ASSOCIATES, DALLAS
TYPOGRAPHIC COMPOSITION: JAGGARS-CHILES-STOVALL, DALLAS; GRAPHIC ARTS TYPOGRAPHERS, NEW YORK, NEW YORK
LITHOGRAPHY: THE STECK COMPANY, AUSTIN
BOOKBINDING: UNIVERSAL BOOKBINDERY, INC., SAN ANTONIO